Praise for *Working 9 to 5*

"A riveting insider tale of how women in offices across America took on their *Mad Men* bosses and won. Part memoir, part blueprint for social change, *Working 9 to 5* brilliantly captures the joy, humor, and creativity of this freewheeling, bold movement."

—**Dorothy Sue Cobble**, author of *For the Many*

"An inspiring story of women who organized for respect on the job."

—**Mary Kay Henry**, international president,
Service Employees International Union (SEIU)

"In these days of hard times for unions and workers, it's good to have Ellen Cassedy to remind us of a struggle that looked pretty hopeless when it started but made a big difference. Women's work is still undervalued and underpaid, so what are we waiting for? Read *Working 9 to 5* for the story of a not-so-distant past that could help us figure out how to make a better, fairer future."

—**Katha Pollitt**, columnist, the *Nation*

"I love a book that combines a powerful story, strategic thinking, and tips for action—and this is a great one!"

—**Elissa McBride**, secretary-treasurer, American Federation of State,
County and Municipal Employees (AFSCME)

"The women of 9 to 5 joined together for respect, recognition, and rights, paving the way for so many of today's organizing efforts for economic and gender justice. It is history we can learn from and be inspired by."

—**Ai-jen Poo**, cofounder and president,
National Domestic Workers Alliance

"[*Working 9 to 5*] provides useful insights as we enter a new era of worker-led movements for change."

—**Sara Steffens**, secretary-treasurer,
Communications Workers of America

"*Working 9 to 5* beautifully tells the story of how 9 to 5's early organizing work was fueled by love, dedication, and a commitment to fighting for essential human rights for working women. Thanks to their groundbreaking work nearly five decades ago, we're still here at the forefront fighting for economic justice, gender justice, and racial justice and protecting the democracy of the people."

—**Leng Leng Chancey**, executive director, 9to5

"Ellen Cassedy has done us all a great favor by skillfully telling the story of this group of trailblazers at the intersection of the women's and labor rights movements. Their story should inspire and motivate us to continue to fight for change and improve working conditions for all."

—**Nicole Korkolis**, director of communication, education, and research, the Office and Professional Employees International Union (OPEIU)

"Anyone who thinks about gender, labor, and equality will be grateful for this comprehensive look at where we've come from and what comes next."

—**Dahlia Lithwick**, senior legal correspondent, *Slate*

"This victory story is one of power building and justice. It will surely teach and motivate today's young organizers and movement leaders."

—**Tiffany Dena Loftin**, senior adviser, Grassroots Law Project

"We at the Fight for $15 stand on the shoulders of women who organized before us. The story of 9 to 5 is inspiring for organizers today!"

—**Ciara Fox**, Wisconsin lead organizer, Fight for $15

"The women of 9 to 5 were gutsy and creative. Their story can inspire a new generation fighting for fair pay and fair treatment."

—**Saru Jayaraman**, president and cofounder, One Fair Wage

"If we organize, we can change the world. This is a detailed and personal view of how a determined group of women organized and achieved more than they ever imagined."

—**Heather Booth**, founder, Midwest Academy

"The women's movement was never limited to its earliest activists. It quickly proliferated and spread to women in all kinds of occupations. Most important was 9 to 5 . . . and they were incredibly successful."

—**Ruth Rosen**, author of *The World Split Open*

"These well-written stories will inspire, motivate, and teach a new generation of organizers to build power."

—**Mary Jean Collins**, historian, Veteran Feminists of America

"An inspiring must-read for union and activist organizers!"

—**Vicki Saporta**, former director of organizing, International Brotherhood of Teamsters

"Cassedy lets us feel the thrill and uncertainty, the courage and verve of the small band of women who spoke the truth they saw, learned to organize, and broke the mold of the obedient secretary."

—**Julia Reichert** and **Steven Bognar**, Academy Award
–winning filmmakers of *9to5: The Story of a Movement* and *American Factory*

"The 9 to 5 movement helped birth the Fight for $15, vibrant domestic workers' organizing, #MeToo, a renewal of union activism, many iterations of feminism, the 2017 anti–Donald Trump Women's March, and the still-too-slow progressive resurgence within the Democratic Party. *Working 9 to 5* tells the story of the heroic yet human women who led this transformative change well and boldly."

—**Joan Walsh**, national affairs correspondent, the *Nation*

"A lively story of women workers coming together in a shared commitment to equal opportunity and justice for all. It is struggles like these that help the eventuality that America will live up to its ideals."

—**Wade Henderson**, former president,
the Leadership Conference on Civil and Human Rights

"*Working 9 to 5* imbues social history with practical knowledge about movement building and the day-to-day work of collective power. The timing for this book couldn't be better."
—**Michelle Miller**, cofounder and co–executive director, Coworker.org

"A lively story with valuable and timely insights into how to build a union."
—**Linda Gordon**, coauthor of *Feminism Unfinished*

"The story of 9 to 5 is a 'how-to guide' for those looking to build a social and economic movement. . . . Working America is an organization that grew out of the leadership spawned by 9 to 5. We can see the lessons of the simple concept of strength in numbers from the voiceless as the guiding principle for thousands of organizers who will build the next great movement."

—**Matt Morrison**, executive director, Working America

"Behind all great advances for justice you will find a group of organizers that moved an idea from the margins to the mainstream to policy. Ellen Cassedy's *Working 9 to 5* masterfully brings an essential thread of history to life."

—**George Goehl**, former executive director, People's Action

"*Working 9 to 5* should be required reading for any organizer seeking to empower workers and change lives."

—**Tom Israel**, program director, center for organizing
and affiliate support, National Education Association

Working
9 to 5

Working 9 to 5

A WOMEN'S MOVEMENT, A LABOR UNION, AND THE ICONIC MOVIE

ELLEN CASSEDY

CHICAGO
REVIEW
PRESS

Copyright © 2022 by Ellen Cassedy
Foreword copyright © 2022 by Jane Fonda
All rights reserved
Published by Chicago Review Press Incorporated
814 North Franklin Street
Chicago, Illinois 60610
ISBN 978-1-64160-822-0

Library of Congress Control Number: 2022935122

Typesetting: Nord Compo

Printed in the United States of America
5 4 3 2 1

The worker must have bread, but she must have roses, too.

—Rose Schneiderman, early twentieth-
century garment worker leader

Working 9 to 5—what a way to make a living!

—Dolly Parton

CONTENTS

Chicago Review Press's house style is to capitalize *White*. Our intent is to signal that Whiteness is not the norm but rather a cultural construct like other cultural categorizations. We feel that not capitalizing *White* can promote the idea that Whiteness is the standard, ordinary, or unraced. We want to emphasize that Whiteness is itself a cultural identity that has implications in our society.

FOREWORD
by Jane Fonda

I'M AN ACTIVIST AS WELL AS AN ACTOR, and at times over the years the two have come together in wonderful ways. That's what happened with 9 to 5.

In the early 1970s, I began hearing from my friends in the 9 to 5 movement about the problems women office workers were facing. I heard about the creative ways they were winning rights and respect on the job— and making bosses get their own coffee.

I decided to make a movie about what I was hearing, and I asked Lily Tomlin and Dolly Parton to join me.

I met with 9 to 5 members of diverse races, classes, and ages—Black, Brown, Asian, White, young and old—and listened closely to their stories. They told me about having to perform demeaning tasks for their bosses. Training men who would then go up the ladder past them while they remained stuck on the lower rungs. Watching their bosses take credit for their ideas. Experiencing race, sex, and age discrimination.

These women worked hard. They did skilled work and knew the office as well as or better than their bosses did. No business could run without them, and they knew it. Their stories—and their fantasies about getting even with the boss—all went into the script.

The movie 9 to 5 was a 1980 box-office hit, and it was these women's stories that made it the success that it was. For the first time, twenty million women office workers could see themselves up on the screen as the centerpiece of a major motion picture. Dolly's catchy, savvy theme song, "9 to 5," became an enduring anthem.

9 to 5 was a comedy with a serious core. Three women get fed up and end up kidnapping their boss. We see what happens when women join together and figure out how to turn their complaints into action. It turns out they can run the company better than their boss ever did.

The movement built the movie, and the movie built the movement. That synergy was thrilling for all of us.

The 9 to 5 women started out as a group of ten office workers in Boston, sitting in a circle and sharing their problems with pay, promotions, and the "pink-collar ghetto." At first no one thought women office workers would go on to organize on a nationwide scale.

But they did.

Their movement was of women, by women, and for women.

All kinds of women found a home in 9 to 5. And maybe the way they organized could *only* have been done by women.

They met at watercoolers, during lunch hours, and sometimes after work with their children in tow. They used their telephones and typewriters to get the message out. They surveyed, leafleted, and petitioned. They lobbied and rallied. They confronted their employers and public officials to demand raises, rights, and respect. Their meetings, their leaflets, and their picket lines were not quite like anything seen before.

Together, they pioneered new strategies for pressuring the powerful and winning a better life on the job. They combined flashy public campaigns with subversive ways for office women to make their voices heard.

They gave expression to concepts like sexual harassment and pregnancy discrimination that at the time had no name and were perfectly legal.

The women of 9 to 5 understood that the issues of economic and racial injustice must be tackled together because they have the same root causes: greed, racism, hubris.

They put the tools of activism into the hands of women workers. And they created a world of new possibilities.

In a few short years, they built a feisty nationwide movement that took on the corporate titans and won millions of dollars in back pay and promotions. They lit a fire under government agencies and strengthened the laws protecting women on the job. They started a woman-led union, inspired hundreds of new women labor organizers, and ushered in a new era of organizing. With thousands of members in two dozen chapters, they transformed workplaces across America. They changed the image of working women and made it clear that women are not secondary, temporary wage earners but workers in their own right, and with rights.

They surprised themselves, and they surprised the world.

Their story will move you and inspire you.

PROLOGUE

On January 21, 2017, the day after Donald Trump was sworn in as president, hundreds of thousands of women gathered in Washington, DC. Packed so tight they could barely move, they filled the streets of the nation's capital. Across the country, an estimated four million people participated in the Women's March that day. Many of them had never taken part in any kind of protest before. It was among the largest demonstrations in US history.

That was the day I decided I had to write the story of 9 to 5. Those women reminded me of the working women—me among them—who joined together in the 1970s to win a better life on the job.

We 9 to 5'ers felt a responsibility to change the world, and we had a growing confidence that it could be done. We built a nationwide multiracial movement that brought pressure to bear on companies that undervalued women and people of color. We invented new strategies for pressuring the banks, insurance companies, law firms, universities, and publishing companies. We filed lawsuits, threw up picket lines, sent out press releases, and leafleted without pause. We strengthened the laws protecting women on the job and got government working to enforce them. We inspired Jane Fonda to make her film and Dolly Parton to write her toe-tapping song.

The union we launched—of women, by women, and for women—propelled thousands of workers into action and won higher pay, better benefits, and a host of improvements. We ran into ferocious opposition from corporations, yet we brought women into the labor movement in lasting ways and charted new directions for worker power.

Some of us called ourselves feminists; others didn't. All of us found ourselves speaking up in ways we'd never imagined. As we put newly learned organizing skills and newly invented tactics into practice, we were transformed. And so were the workplaces of America. We won raises, rights, and respect for millions of women. The offices of America have not been the same since.

For a new generation facing new challenges and fueled by new passions—for anyone striving for fair treatment—the story of 9 to 5 proves that change can be won, and it shows how we won it.

Recently I came across a quotation on a little scrap of paper that I used to keep on my desk at the 9 to 5 office. "Through our great good fortune," it says, "in our youth our hearts were touched with fire."

That's what it was like for me and all of us in the 9 to 5 movement. This is our story.

Some of the names of the office workers who told their stories in the early days of the 9 to 5 movement were changed to protect their identities.

1

EVERY MORNING

"GET YOUR 9 TO 5 newsletter! Get your *9 to 5!*"

The highest windows along the Boston skyline were beginning to brighten as I stood shivering outside a subway stop on an early December morning in 1972. I was twenty-two, one of a group of ten young women who had spread out across the city that morning to distribute our crisply folded broadside to as many office workers as we could.

From below came a rumble and a rush of wind that smelled of dirt, sweat, and motor oil. Up the stairs came a stampede of boots and coats and faces, women headed for executive suites and typing pools, small firms and giant corporations, stuffy back offices and gleaming glass towers. For the next eight hours, they would file, collate, mimeograph, staple, stuff, type, address, punch, seal, alphabetize, transcribe, photocopy—and find a few minutes, I hoped, to look at the newsletter I was pressing into their hands with my frozen fingers.

"Every morning, thousands of us—mostly women—get up, dress up, and go off to work in the offices of Boston," read the article on the front page. "We keep Boston's businesses and institutions running smoothly. Without us, they would grind to a halt. Yet we are underpaid and undervalued."

At that point, the first pink "pussy hat" hadn't yet been knitted for the 2017 Women's March, and the #MeToo movement against sexual misconduct in the workplace was years in the future, but something was afoot. As office work—"the business of doing business"—moved rapidly

9to5

newsletter for boston area office workers

VOL. 1, NO. 1   DECEMBER 72/ JANUARY 73

Every Morning...

Every morning thousands of us - mostly women - get up, dress up, and go off to work in the offices of Boston. In business corporations, hospitals, and universities, we file, collate, mimeograph, staple, stuff, type, address, punch, seal, alphabetize, transcribe, and Xerox the material that arrives at our desks. We deal in paper, recording and communicating the activities of others. Our jobs are largely mechanical; the skills we use don't require much understanding of the workings of the institutions we serve. Yet we are as essential in our places of employment as the cooks in a restaurant or the welders on an auto assembly line. We keep Boston's businesses and institutions running smoothly. Without us, they would grind to a halt.

Yet most clerical workers have very little decision-making power at our jobs. Rare indeed is an office in which all the secretaries get together to rotate work and share responsibilities. Nor do we help to determine the overall policies of the institutions we work for. Denied the opportunity to think about what we are doing and make changes, we are often bored. And our importance is also unrecognized materially; we are paid very little and receive few benefits.

How do we deal with this situation? Many of us try to play down the discouraging aspects of our jobs. We don't define ourselves as office workers - for example, we think of ourselves more as mothers or wives. Yet this image doesn't reflect reality.

(continued on page 2)

We handed out our *9 to 5* newsletter all over Boston. *Schlesinger Library, Harvard Radcliffe Institute (top) and Author's collection (bottom)*

to the center of the economy, the clerical workforce was growing by leaps and bounds, and discontent among its mostly female members was on the rise. A few years later, in the blockbuster movie inspired by our movement, Jane Fonda and her costars would bring that discontent to life on the big screen.

Most women working in offices hadn't been part of the women's liberation movement of the 1960s. They hadn't joined in the iconic protest at the Miss America contest in Atlantic City in 1968 (where bras either were or were not burned—accounts differ). They might not have heard about the Women's Strike for Equality that took place in multiple cities on August 26, 1970, the fiftieth anniversary of women winning the vote. They weren't active in the ongoing campaign for the ratification of the Equal Rights Amendment. Many of them rejected the label *feminist* or *women's libber*. They might not have used the word *discrimination*. But they wanted to be treated fairly and compensated equally on the job. These workplace goals were part of the women's movement from the start. In fact, equal pay was the movement's first rallying cry. In the offices of America, that cry was passed from office worker to office worker, cubicle to cubicle. As historian Dorothy Sue Cobble put it, "The messages of the new feminism stirred discontent" among office workers far and wide.

I was one of those office workers. I'd graduated from college the year before and discovered that the only jobs I could find to support myself were waitressing and office work. My best friend from college, Karen Nussbaum, was working as a clerk-typist at Harvard University, and when a position opened up in her department, I took it. It was Karen who had the idea of getting a group together to talk about our jobs. Ten of us who worked in a variety of offices—friends and friends of friends—began meeting weekly in one another's homes to share our experiences.

Karen had her stories. There was the professor who passed her in the hall while she was carrying a heavy load of dissertations and asked, "Why aren't you smiling?" And the male student who marched in, looked her right in the eye, and asked, "Isn't anybody here?" I had my stories too. There was the time my boss came down the hall to ask me to remove a calendar from his wall. I dutifully followed him back down the hall to his office and removed the calendar—something he could have done all by himself in five seconds. Why hadn't he? Much worse was the philosophy professor who hired me to come to his apartment and transcribe a sheaf of handwritten notes, which turned out to be a detailed account of all the blow jobs he'd ever received. When I sat down at the typewriter, he took off his shirt and stood before me bare chested, waiting for . . . what? I knew what was going on was wrong, and scary, but I had no vocabulary for it and didn't know what to do. Heart pounding, I started typing.

Our group would sit in a circle and talk not only about ourselves but about our coworkers too. Some of our coworkers were middle-aged women who had worked in offices for years. Others were young women straight out of high school. Some had professional secretarial skills; others had degrees in English literature. Many were seething. We heard complaints like these:

After eight years, I'm still at the bottom of the pay scale.

I trained a man to be my supervisor.

I have a degree in communications, but all they asked me to do was take a typing test.

It began to dawn on us that we had our finger on the pulse of a giant and growing sector of the American workforce, one that had long been ignored. Aside from the stereotypes of secretaries as either officious gatekeepers or airheaded bimbos, women who worked in offices were strangely invisible. When people thought "worker," they pictured a man in a hard hat or a welder on an assembly line. Yet now the economy was changing. New economic conditions and new cultural expectations were pulling women into the workforce by the millions. One in three was an office worker. Nationwide, women's pay was less than 60 percent of men's—a bigger gap than in the 1950s. For non-White women, the figure was only 54 percent. We didn't know what we wanted to do, but we had dreams. Could we form a union? A citywide organization? Maybe something even bigger?

An evening of brainstorming had yielded the name "9 to 5," reflecting the hours of the workday, and now our newsletter was getting out into the world. It offered firsthand reports from the front lines of office work. Personal testimonials about what it was like to be a clerk-typist, a secretary, a data entry operator, a receptionist. Cartoons. Archival engravings of the nineteenth-century office. Reports on how bosses responded when asked for a raise. Accounts of small rebellions.

The newsletter, we felt sure, was just our opening act.

There was a lull in the crowd coming up the stairs from the subway—known in Boston as the "T." In an attempt to warm up, I stuffed my hands in the pockets of my coat, a fake suede garment from a thrift store that tended to stiffen in the cold like a board, and stamped my feet in my secondhand boots. A moment later, the tide of workers came rushing up again, and I stepped back into position.

In those days, leafleting was a skill you had to master if you were bent on changing the world. You cradled the stack in the crook of your arm with the folded edges facing out, plucked from the pile, and aimed at the midriffs of the women cresting the stairs. The faster you got the job done, the sooner you could go and have breakfast.

When all my copies were gone, I started out across the Boston Common, past the gleaming gold dome of the State House, the tidy brick buildings of Back Bay, the swan boats in the Public Garden. In Copley Square, I pushed open the door of Ken's, our favorite diner, and inhaled the steamy smells of coffee, toast, and eggs. Karen was already there, her face hidden behind the *Globe*. I was trying to get myself to read the paper every day the way she did. So much was happening—Watergate, the war in Vietnam, the Boston school desegregation crisis.

The waitress looked daggers at us as she took our order. She knew we always asked for the cheapest meal, the no. 1—a small juice, one egg, a slice of toast, and coffee, all for $1.05—and then lingered forever over our refills.

When the food arrived, Karen pulled an envelope from her bag and unfolded a flyer and an application form. "Six-week summer school in Chicago for women organizers," I read. "Tools that will help women vie for power. . . . Through conscious organization, we can win the rights that should be ours. . . .Tuition $500. Apply to the Midwest Academy by April 15."

Wasn't this just what our group needed? We were full of hopes and dreams, but we were aware that we didn't know how to "win the rights that should be ours," and we were eager for answers.

"So are you going?" I asked.

"I was thinking you should," she said.

I set down my cup with a clatter. Me instead of her? Why? I knew the answer, though. Classrooms made her antsy. Not long after we'd met in college, she'd dropped out to join the antiwar movement. I opposed the war too. I went to mass meetings and I blocked the university gates during the student strike. But I also wanted an education. I wanted to read philosophy, study French, sharpen my wits with math assignments, try to get good grades. I loved being a student.

I folded the flyer and put it in my bag. "I'll think about it," I said. I had to get to my cubicle at Harvard.

Karen shrugged on her coat, navy blue with toggles, and hefted her bag onto her shoulder. "Do it," she said. She was out the door.

A few nights later I sat down at the kitchen table at the house on Wendell Street that I shared with eight other people. While one of my housemates washed the dishes, I spread out the materials from the training school. My fellow 9 to 5'ers had endorsed the idea of sending me to Chicago, and my boss had granted me a two-month leave while the campus was mostly shut down for the summer. During this time, he'd have to deal with the wall calendar on his own.

I'd written college applications when I was in high school, but this one was different. No grade point average, no test scores. Instead, "Describe your most recent organizational work," said the first question. That was easy. Recently a group of us office workers at Harvard had asked for a meeting with the director of personnel. We'd rehearsed for weeks, but even so we were terrified as we presented our list of demands, including higher pay. To our amazement, the director was terrified too. His hands were trembling. I wrote all about the meeting on the form, but I had to admit that none of our demands had been met.

"Please attach your résumé," said the form—your *movement* résumé, that is. Why exactly *was* I interested in getting trained to "vie for power," anyway?

My boyfriend, Jeff Blum, would know what I should say. With years of leading student protests under his belt, he'd have plenty of advice to offer. I was trying not to call him, though. This morning, as I got ready for work, he'd buried himself in the covers in my bed and gone back to sleep. His job at Boston City Hospital didn't start till noon.

"I love you," he'd mumbled as I was on my way out the door.

I bent down for a kiss. "See you tonight?"

No answer. He turned over and hugged the pillow. I felt a familiar prickle of anxiety. We'd been going out for a year, and we were definitely a couple, but . . . would it last? Were we right for each other? Is this what a serious relationship was supposed to feel like?

A few days earlier he'd complained that I was "too hard-nosed." I thought I was too soft. I was trying to be as tough as Karen, or at least tougher than I was, anyway. But maybe Jeff was right. Maybe I needed to loosen up.

When I asked Karen what she thought, she was blunt. "Tell him to shove it," she said.

What would Jeff do—and with whom?—if I left Boston and went to Chicago for the summer?

Back to my movement résumé. I had an activist heritage of a sort. My grandfather, who had grown up studying religious texts in a little town in Lithuania, used to tell about how he'd had his eyes opened to politics. He remembered a young man with red hair—like mine—who'd turned him into an activist. It was because of this redhead that my grandfather spent several years running up and down the stairs of New York tenement buildings in the early twentieth century, distributing flyers for socialist candidates. My parents were politically active too. They took me to demonstrations for peace and civil rights, including a picket line for fair housing when a landlord in our mostly White community refused to rent to a Black family. In 1963, in junior high school, I spent my lunch hours collecting money for the March on Washington, the groundbreaking demonstration led by Dr. Martin Luther King Jr., and I helped found a group called SNAP—Student Nonviolent Action for Peace.

In high school, when the siren sounded for the periodic air raid shelter drills that were supposed to protect us in the case of a nuclear attack, I'd hurry to put on the armband I kept in my pencil holder. THE ONLY

SHELTER IS PEACE was its message, and when we were herded into the hall, I refused to face the wall and was sent to the principal's office. I wrote passionate articles for the school newspaper calling out the misogyny and general stupidity of the health ed curriculum. (Among the health "facts" on a mimeographed sheet we received: "Menstruation is the special burden of the woman and she must accept her lot," and "Females inspect their nails by pointing their fingernails away from them; males curl their fingers inward.")

Shortly after I entered college in 1968, the campus exploded with protests against the Vietnam War, the university's mistreatment of the surrounding Black community, and other grievances. At first, I felt acutely annoyed. I was being asked, it seemed, to choose between studying and caring about the world. I didn't want to choose. In time, though, a synthesis emerged. I could study *and* care about the world. Women's studies became part of the academic curriculum, and our instructors excitedly shared the buried stories of women they were discovering in their research. The spirit in the classrooms was electric, every seat taken and auditors lining the walls. I joined a women's consciousness-raising group on campus, read *The Feminine Mystique* and *Sisterhood Is Powerful*, began calling my friends "women" instead of "girls." And I wrote my senior thesis about immigrant women who'd fought for their rights in the mills and sweatshops at the turn of the twentieth century.

All of this was eye-opening, and so was my realization, as graduation drew near, that while I'd grown up expecting to excel in the classroom, somehow I'd never felt it necessary to prepare for a career. I had not a clue about what to do with all the knowledge I'd gained—either my liberal arts learning or my new insights into women's place in society. I knew I was supposed to get married and raise a family. But beyond that . . . well, I hoped something would work out.

After graduation, when Karen invited me to move to Boston, I thought, "Why not?" In 1971 it was easy for people like me to move to a new place, find a cheap place to live, and get some kind of job, so long as we weren't too picky. Activism was Karen's career. She knew what she was doing. If I stuck by her side, I figured I'd end up doing something that mattered. And sure enough, here I was, helping to put out a terrific newsletter and to make bosses, or at least the personnel director at Harvard, tremble.

Now, sitting at the kitchen table with the organizer school application, I felt ready for more, ready to get out from under Karen's wing, step up, step out, and try my own wings. Maybe I could move on from being simply a participant, a follower. Maybe this summer training could help me find my way—my calling.

At the turn of the twentieth century, women in the mills and garment factories had organized by the hundreds of thousands. I loved their anthem, "Bread and Roses," which began:

> As we come marching, marching, in the beauty of the day
> A million darkened kitchens, a thousand mill lofts gray
> Are touched with all the radiance that a sudden sun discloses
> For the people hear us singing, bread and roses, bread and roses

Today it was no longer mill workers but office workers who held the low-paid, low-status jobs at the center of our changing economy. Maybe now it was our turn to add a link to the chain of social change that stretched back through the generations. And maybe I could be part of forging that link.

2

VYING FOR POWER

At the school for organizers, I took notes at a furious pace. I was glad to be back in a classroom, and this time around I felt I might well be preparing myself for a career. Also, the 9 to 5'ers back home were counting on me, and I was determined not to let them down.

"Organizers build democracy," I scribbled. "Organizers inspire people to think and act in ways they never dared. Organizing is the art of getting people together and helping them build structures through which to express their concerns and improve their lives."

I loved Heather Booth, the main teacher. On the very first day, with her cap of dark hair and her lime blouse tucked crisply into navy slacks, she looked strong and smart, and also warm. How sure of herself she seemed! As a college student, she'd been among the thousands of northern students—most of them White like her—who went down to Mississippi in the summer of 1964 to help southern civil rights activists register Black people to vote. On campus, she'd fought for women's rights and an end to the Vietnam War. When the student movement splintered and petered out, she saw a need for another kind of activism and studied with the veteran community leader Saul Alinsky to learn new ways to mobilize people in the 1970s. Alinsky was renowned for organizing people in low-income communities, using public embarrassment and the threat of mass unrest to win concessions from the powers that be. But Alinsky didn't place much value on training women organizers, Heather found. So she decided to take on that job herself.

"Women have been the backbone of most organizations," she wrote. "They make the phone calls, lick the stamps, ring the doorbells." Yet because women occupy few of the leadership roles, she went on, "many of the real concerns of these women are not put into the programs." Heather thought big: "We want to reach out and join with most women. We cannot be talking about a few hundred or even thousands, but millions."

The brand-new Midwest Academy was the first step toward reaching those millions, and we eighteen women and two men were the first students. All day, from nine in the morning till after dinner, we were instructed in the ABCs of organizing.

I was terrible at all of it.

Used to being an A student in school, here I was at best—at *best*—a C. In a role play where I was assigned to play the mayor of Gary, Indiana, trying to wring concessions out of the board of U.S. Steel, I couldn't open my mouth. When we were sent out into a neighborhood to raise money for a consumer group, all I collected in two hours of door knocking was a measly six dollars. I don't know what I'd expected "vying for power" to be about, but my heart sank at the notion that this might be it.

My fellow students were a lot better at it than I was. Most were older, more confident, more poised. Some were leaders of the National Organization for Women, the feminist group founded in 1966, which boasted tens of thousands of members. Others worked for unions or lobbying organizations, or were part of the nationwide campaign for the Equal Rights Amendment. They were used to making decisions, speaking in public, traveling to new cities, starting new chapters.

In comparison, I was young and green. The main thing I knew how to do in meetings, I realized, was to pick up on people's hesitations and bring them out into the open. "I'm confused," I would say when I saw that other people were confused. Bringing up the rear with the stragglers, I left it to others to lead the way. Leading from behind, you might call it. It was something I did without thinking, a valuable technique that we 9 to 5'ers would refine and use to great effect over the years. But it wasn't enough. To move from being simply a participant to being an organizer, I needed to learn how to do other things as well.

One thing I wasn't quite so terrible at was singing. In between lectures and role plays, we joined hands and belted out the lyrics to Helen Reddy's new hit song:

> I am woman, hear me roar
> . . . .
> I am strong
> I am invincible
> I am woman!

For a few days, we sang "The Internationale," with its stirring first lines:

> Arise, ye prisoners of starvation!
> Arise, ye wretched of the earth
> For justice thunders condemnation
> A better world's in birth!

Then some of the students complained that they didn't feel comfortable singing a socialist anthem. Nor did they like the gospel hymn that moved me deeply:

> We are soldiers in the army
> We got to fight, although we got to cry
> We got to hold up the bloodstained banner
> We got to hold it up until we die

Clearly, we were going to need some new songs. Back then, we couldn't have imagined that Dolly Parton would end up would writing one of them—and that it would shoot to the top of the charts.

Everyone had a one-on-one meeting with Heather, and I proudly brought a stack of our newsletters to mine. I watched as she turned the pages.

"Very nice," she said.

I beamed.

In the pause that followed, I understood that she thought the newsletters were actually kind of pitiful. All they offered was an opportunity to complain. They did nothing to get women joining, moving, winning.

A couple of days later, Steve Max, the other teacher, sat down with me to underscore the point. 9 to 5 was operating on the "rock pile theory," he said, and that would never get us anywhere. The point was not to get people into a meeting room one by one—to pile them up and keep them there until it was time to figure out how to move forward. Instead, we should start by *doing* something—something effective. When people heard about it, they'd come flocking, eager to join in.

Our meeting with the personnel director at Harvard? Yes, it had been something, but not something effective. Sure, the man's hands were trembling, but so what? We should have demanded something we could actually win and then let everyone know about our victory. Steve said we should focus on three goals:

- To win *reforms* that improve people's daily lives.
- To make sure that when people win reforms, they see those gains as rights they've achieved through *their own collective power*.
- To *alter* existing relations of power, weaken the domination of the few, and strengthen the hand of the many.

I wrote it all down.

Back and forth I went between the room I'd rented in someone's sweltering apartment on the South Side of the city and the church basement on the North Side where Heather and Steve imparted their wisdom. Through the bus window, I stared out at the hugeness of Chicago, the big, noisy metropolis that the poet Carl Sandburg had dubbed "Hog Butcher for the World":

Tool Maker, Stacker of Wheat,
Player with Railroads and the Nation's Freight Handler;
Stormy, husky, brawling,
City of the Big Shoulders

The river rolled by, crowded with barges, followed by giant industrial lots that went on for acres. Then came the Loop, the financial district, with its mile after mile of buildings full of women workers, all waiting to be organized.

A letter arrived from Jeff, who'd driven me to the Boston airport for my flight to Chicago. After watching my plane take off, he wrote, "I felt very spacy, like I was floating. I wanted to take you in my arms, sing to you, play the harmonica, break out crying for joy, love you/love you/love you."

Very sweet—more affectionate than he usually acted. To my surprise, I found I wasn't particularly interested. I folded up the letter and put it away.

A few days later came another letter in the same vein: "I love you very much," he wrote, "more than I can really express. It's like a flower opening up in my heart."

And a third: "I've been getting avider and avider waiting for the mail to come. You must be very engrossed in what you're doing."

Maybe he really missed me. Wasn't that what I wanted? I couldn't get myself to write back, though. I wasn't sure how to become an organizer and be a girlfriend at the same time.

He kept trying. A tube of Cuban Revolution posters arrived in the mail, along with an inspirational quotation from Lenin: "Revolutions are festivals of the oppressed and the exploited." I rolled the posters back into their tube and put Lenin aside. I was in another mode now, trying to master Heather and Steve's win-some-reforms-right-now approach.

Jeff and I had gotten to know each other a year and a half earlier, in the storefront office of the antiwar organization to which Karen had recruited us both. In fact, without knowing it, we'd been following each other around the country for years before we finally met. We lived in the same city as children, went to the same college, and moved to Boston at the same time. I liked his grin, the wavy dark hair that flopped into his eyes, his soft flannel shirts and jeans, even his flashy turquoise ring. He was warm, excitable, always engaged. Whenever someone in our noisy, chaotic office called out a question, he always jumped in with an answer. Sometimes, for a goof, he'd answer in high school French, which I found charming. In this hothouse of political fervor, I did my best to keep my own knowledge of French under wraps, afraid of appearing too bourgeois. (As if anyone was fooled.) Jeff was not afraid.

One afternoon as we were hitchhiking up Mass Avenue after work, to my delight he asked me out. We set the date for a few days later, following an evening meeting our group had called to plan a march. As was common in those days, the planning meeting was open to the public, and members of a rival political group showed up in force to argue that the march was a bad idea. The storefront was packed with a hundred people sitting on the floor and on top of the desks. The air was thick with cigarette smoke. Talk, talk, and more talk. Our group wouldn't call off the march and the other group wouldn't back down. Jeff was sitting across the room, not making eye contact. The dinner hour was long past. Would he call off the date? Had he forgotten all about it?

When the meeting ended hours later with the march still in the works but with a change of route, the two of us walked out together. The date was still on, relocated to Jeff's kitchen in the frame two-decker he shared with four or five other people. There he ceremoniously showed me to a seat, brought two bowls of prune yogurt to the table, and sprinkled wheat germ on top. He'd made the yogurt himself, and it was awful—grainy and sour. Nonetheless, I was touched.

The romance began right away and quickly became intense, as we tested out what it was to be intimate, what it was to please and be pleased, to fail to please or be pleased. We pushed ourselves and each other to be direct and forthright. Sometimes we failed. Sometimes we succeeded too much, and honesty got in the way of kindness. One moment we were caring and tender; the next we were locked in a stubborn conflict. What did we want? Independence or interdependence? No matter how difficult things got, though, we didn't break up. We both wanted the back-and-forth, the intensive engagement. Nothing seemed more important.

After just a couple of weeks in Chicago, though, all of that seemed like something out of another life. I tried remembering the getaway we'd had a couple of months earlier, when we drove to West Virginia for a long weekend. We passed the hours on the highway playing word games. I'd been brought up to be tuned in to words—my family kept a shelf of dictionaries in the dining room, and we could rarely get through a meal without discussing a vital matter such as the preferred way to pronounce the word *basil* or the difference between *lie* and *lay*—but Jeff stumped me easily, and I was impressed. Outside the window, the trees were turning pale green, the redbuds a delicate pink. At night we pulled off a winding road, folded down the rear seat of the station wagon, and unrolled a sleeping bag just big enough for the two of us. In the morning when we woke up, the sun was just beginning to burn the mist off the steamy windows, and we were together in a magical bower of leaves. Now it all seemed impossibly far away.

When I finally managed to write back, I sent not a love letter but a report on my training. I described my desire to be strong and self-respecting and went into detail about wanting to keep my insecurities and doubts to myself . . . hence my reluctance to share much about . . . and my inability to tell him about . . . and more along the same lines.

Heather and Steve began to prepare us for going out into the field. Basic training. Boot camp. I was told to wear a watch, to make a daily to-do list, to carry a notebook and a stack of index cards. Part of organizing, it turned out, was being organized.

Maybe the reason I'd raised only six dollars going door-to-door, someone suggested, was the way I looked. I packed away my T-shirts, my blue jeans, and the baggy corduroy jacket I loved. I went to a department store and bought the cheapest respectable-looking outfit I could find, a red-white-and-blue checked rayon top with a matching skirt. I hated it. Worse yet, I walked into a hair salon and had my mop of red curls chopped off. My new do was so severe that I could barely stand to look at myself in the mirror. But if that's what it took . . .

Three or four of us were assigned to a women workers' outreach project called Women Employed, housed at the Chicago YWCA. Our job would be to leave leaflets in ladies' rooms in office buildings and approach women in public parks and company cafeterias during their lunch hours. Heather demonstrated how an organizer should move through the lunch line. Be loud, she said. Attract attention. "Macaroni and cheese *again*?"

"What's in this salad, anyway?" We were even told what to eat—coffee, pie, or a small sandwich—in order to leave the maximum time for conversation. Our instructions were:

- Maintain eye contact.
- If you're nervous, remember they are too.
- Keep your goal in mind. You want them to come to a meeting.

Keeping a goal in mind—that was a new one for me. Somehow it hadn't occurred to me that you needed a plan for everything, even a conversation in the park. It all seemed very strange.

Out into the financial canyons we went. We prowled like spies through the palatial department stores and strolled into cafeterias and employee lounges as if we belonged there. Hearts pounding, we breezed by the guards in the lobbies of big insurance companies. We scurried into bathrooms and left stacks of leaflets on the windowsills and counters.

Most of the women I approached in the company cafeterias brushed me off, but once in a while I managed to get someone to talk to me. A department store employee named Diane allowed me to join her at her lunch table, where she let loose with a long list of gripes about her low pay, her boorish supervisor, and her skimpy vacation. Her coworkers were as unhappy as she was, she said. Keeping my goal in mind, I suggested that she distribute our flyers and bring some of her friends to meet me for lunch the following week. She said she would. I was thrilled.

But the next time I called her, she told me she'd decided not to pass out the flyers after all, and she didn't set up the meeting. I never saw her again.

Another day, I spent an hour at a table with a group of women who whipped themselves into a bitter froth of indignation. Then they went back to work, and . . . well, now what? Steve told me I should have interrupted their rant to ask, "Have you talked to other employees about these problems? What did you decide to do?" If all they wanted to do was complain, I should have brought the encounter to a close.

Every Wednesday, we held a collective lunch meeting for everyone we'd met during the week. I invited Debby, Joyce, Lydia, and Kay. None of them came. What was I doing wrong? "You should have called them that morning to remind them," Steve said, "and you should have enticed them with something urgent you were going to be talking about."

Steve and I talked in detail about everyone I met. People were so complicated. And they had so many excuses for not coming to a meeting. Susan had a church meeting every Wednesday. Brenda was moving to New York. Laverne worked till seven o'clock. All of this on top of the big reasons, the real reasons—fear of getting fired, fear of change, fear of looking silly in the eyes of coworkers, fear that none of it would amount to anything.

"Be patient," Steve said. "You'll have to eat a lot of lunches to get one or two women to come to a meeting." He assured me I'd get the hang of it.

I wasn't so certain.

I'd been in Chicago for about a month when Jeff came to town. He and three friends had long been preparing for a backpacking expedition in the Wyoming wilderness, and now they were on their way out west. Here he was—long hair, hiking boots, turquoise ring, and all. He was loaded down with provisions—boots, tentpoles, canteens, bags of grains and dried fruit. And he was fascinated by what I was learning and eager to hear all about it.

At first I held back. My new knowledge and my new skills were fragile, and I was afraid that if I exposed them to Jeff's scrutiny, I'd end up feeling that I hadn't learned much after all, or had learned the wrong things. If I let myself sink into being a girlfriend, I feared I'd lose my momentum and be unable to stick with learning how to lure Diane and Laverne to an after-work meeting. By the end of a few days, though, I loosened up and felt glad to be with him.

During the visit, his mother called to say his father was back in the hospital with the kidney ailment he'd been battling. Jeff considered canceling the trip, but in the end he set off for the outback as planned. I went back to my labors in the Loop.

Five years earlier, Grant Park was where police had clubbed anti-war protesters during the 1968 Democratic National Convention. Now at lunchtime all was serene on the park's green lawns. Women with sandwiches sat in twos and threes on benches under the trees. Each day, with a clipboard under my arm, I'd stand for a moment gathering my courage, then plunge in.

"Hi, we're taking a survey of women's jobs. Can you talk for a few minutes?"

Two women who worked at a giant oil company told me they couldn't think of a single thing they didn't like about their jobs. Then I asked about their salaries.

"I've been on the job for seventeen months," the first one said, "and I still haven't gotten a raise. I only make $525 a month."

The second one gasped. "You do? I only make $490!"

After that, more problems came pouring out, and I walked away practically skipping with joy. Then my footsteps slowed. I'd forgotten all about having a goal. I hadn't asked them to come to a meeting or even gotten their names.

I was determined to do better. The next day, the first woman I approached said she didn't want to talk because she was eating her lunch. That was par for the course, but as I was turning away, I heard her next words: "And besides, I don't really care."

I felt like slapping her. I lay down on the grass, pressed my face into the earth, and escaped it all by falling asleep.

A few days later, Jeff called from Baltimore with the news that his father had died while he was hiking. Now he was home with his mother, grieving and bitterly regretting having gone on the trip. Later I received a letter he'd mailed from Wyoming as he'd gotten on the plane to go home. Inside was a poem:

> Wind rustling through trees
> Blowing hard up the canyon
> I want to share this with you
> The rushing stream
> The ever-changing wind
> I want to be with you

And with this wind,
This sun beating
This hard and soft and varied earth . . .

I struggled to put myself in his place, to understand what he'd felt
out in the wilderness and what he was going through now in the wake of
his father's death. I couldn't really manage it. I put the letter in a drawer.
I had work to do.

By the end of the summer, I'd filled two notebooks. I wasn't a super-
organizer yet. Maybe I wasn't an organizer at all. But I expected more of
myself. I was no longer satisfied with being a follower. I wanted to help
set a direction. I was a bit more confident, and better at getting on with
whatever I was supposed to be doing, even when it felt hard. I could take
a deep breath and march into the ladies' room at an insurance company,
or accost a woman in a cafeteria I wasn't supposed to be in, or approach
a stranger in the park.

Heather and Steve gave me some parting advice. Be more audacious,
they said, less transparent. Be open and human, but stay on task. And,
Heather added, in addition to keeping my hair cut short and trying to
dress like the rest of the downtown workforce, I should consider carrying a
lipstick in my purse. "You never know when you might need it," she said.

As I was packing for home, someone from the 9 to 5 group called
me in tears. My friends had sent me off to find out how to turn our cozy
group into something big and effective. Now they were scared. What was
I going to do to them when I got back?

I understood their anxiety. I was scared too. Would I be able to lead
them to a new place? Would they be able to follow?

At the graduation ceremony, there were speeches and rounds of
applause, photographs and hugs, and a freshly composed anthem scribbled
by a couple of the students:

Action is the key to power
If you want to win

There's a school that teaches tactics
It's where we begin!

It was night when my plane took off. The lights of the Loop disappeared, replaced by the black expanse of Lake Michigan. In my suitcase
I carried my notebooks full of knowledge. Ahead lay Boston, where all
that I'd learned would be put to the test.

3

START-UP

BEFORE MEETING WITH MY 9 TO 5 FRIENDS, I gave myself a pep talk. "Be more aggressive," I wrote in my notebook, and underlined the words in red. *Speak loudly and clearly*, I told myself. *Ban the word* confused *from your vocabulary. Stop looking over your shoulder to see what Karen thinks. Take responsibility.*

All ten of us were jittery as we settled into chairs and sofas at Karen's house. I'd brought notes to help me with my presentation. At first the circle of familiar faces looked tentative, but as I kept talking, I could see people opening up. To grow and be effective, I told my friends, we needed an office and a staff. Becoming a strong voice for Boston's two hundred thousand women office workers would require more than a volunteer effort. I had only a few hundred dollars to my name, but I proposed to quit my clerk-typist job at Harvard, and the group vowed to raise money for my salary. My new career as an organizer began to take off.

Over the previous year, we'd collected a slim stack of names—readers of our newsletter who'd sent in tear-off coupons or written us letters. But as my teacher Steve had made clear, it would be a mistake to pull in these new people right away, before we knew what to do with them. Before reaching out, we needed a plan for action, a plan to catapult the concerns of office workers into the public eye, a plan to engage "the enemy" by making demands on employers.

Excitement built in the room as we decided to spend the month of September getting in touch with leaders of other women's groups, union leaders, discrimination lawyers, professors—anyone who might be able to help us understand the world of office work in Boston. We'd then spend October meeting as many office workers as we could and inviting them to participate in a November event where we'd unveil our agenda. At that point we would have created a new organization, one that could absorb new members and propel them into action.

After the meeting, Karen offered me a ride home, but I wanted to walk up Mass Avenue by myself. I wanted to be alone, to savor the moment, to pat myself on the back for surmounting this first hurdle, and to absorb the amazing reality that we might actually be on our way toward getting something off the ground.

I was still feeling exultant when I got to Jeff's shared house, where I was staying for now. My own group house had broken up over the summer while I was away. Jeff was in Baltimore with his mother, still atoning for having gone into the outback while his father lay dying. In the front hall, the ceiling light had burned out, and I had to feel my way into Jeff's room, which was bare except for the mattress on the floor and my clothes in a heap in the corner. The one bathroom was occupied, and someone was sobbing on the one phone while loud voices filled the kitchen. Eight people were more than enough for this house. I'd have to find a new place soon. But first, 9 to 5 needed an office.

A couple of days later, I set off for the downtown business district to scout for a place. After Chicago, Boston looked like a toy city—miniature, antique. For decades now, the biggest businesses in the city had been producers not of things but of services—finance, research, education, technology. Unlike Chicago with its robust industrial economy, its barges and foundries and meatpacking plants, Boston ran on a paper economy, with office work and office workers at its core.

I headed in the direction of the new John Hancock Tower, the flagship of the financial sector, taller than all the rest and striking in its all-glass beauty. Partially occupied but still under construction, it was already plagued with problems. When the wind blew, the building swayed so much that people on the upper floors felt sick. Also, for reasons no one could figure out, the beautiful blue windows were shattering. Pea-sized nuggets of glass crunched underfoot on the sidewalks surrounding the tower, and guards had been posted to peer up into the sky with binoculars, ready to shoo pedestrians away whenever a new pane started to blow. I still have one of those little pieces of glass. For years, I carried it in my purse as an amulet, a sign that the mighty could be brought low.

Behind the Hancock, and dwarfed by it, stood the red-brick YWCA, where I had an appointment to talk about renting a room. Formerly a residence for single women, the building now housed a day care center, an art studio, and vocational classrooms. Of the thirteen stories, many were now vacant, including one with a pool with a cracked floor that hadn't been used in years.

I followed a noisy crowd of three-year-olds through the dim lobby into the elevator, which was operated by a man with a hand crank—an anachronism even back then. For my meeting with the director, I'd prepared a speech about how much I loved the Y and was awed by its motto (One Imperative: Eliminate Racism), but she cut me off midsentence and briskly escorted me to a tiny room with a frosted glass door and two battered wooden desks. Outside the window, the Hancock building loomed, so close you could practically touch it. For a hundred dollars a month, the room was ours.

Not that we had a hundred dollars. So although the office couldn't have been bigger than twelve feet by twelve feet square, we put out a call for a cotenant to share the room. A lawyer who'd filed a discrimination suit against the City of Boston moved in, along with her colleague, a former city employee who regaled us with stories about battles for fair employment, including one about her sister being arrested for biting a police officer.

Giddy with exhilaration, I set up shop at one of the desks. A few weeks later Karen cut down her hours at Harvard and joined me. We kept the radio on. The Watergate scandal was in full swing, and Nixon was going down. My usually mild-mannered mother wrote me: "Watergate. I devour every detail. God, how I love it. I have a lovely fantasy that Nixon will be impeached and everyone will line the streets as he's carried away in a cart, and jeers and taunts will fill the air, and I will be there where he can see me, and I'll stick my tongue out, and he will know at last that I hate him. Love, Moth." (Yes, her characteristic sign-off was "Moth," short for Mother.)

The space was much too tight. We tried rearranging the desks in various configurations, but nothing helped. One morning, Karen and I spotted an upright piano sitting in the hallway and lost no time rolling it into the office between the two desks. Then we hid nearby and waited for our fellow tenants, the lawyer and her sidekick, to arrive. As they struggled to push open the door, we exploded in giggles. The lawyer's long-suffering sigh just made us laugh harder.

Juvenile? Absolutely. As we met with the people on our list of potential helpers, we were aware that they were all older than we were. They were adults, and we were glad. Too often, the history of organizing in America has been stop and start, with little contact between the activists of different eras. But we wanted to reach across the generational divide. We knew we wouldn't just be continuing the work of these elders. We'd have to forge our own path. Even so, we were eager to learn from those who'd come before.

Some of those we met with took one look at our twenty-three-year-old selves and said, either kindly or not so kindly, "Forget it, kids. We've tried it all before. It didn't work." Others seemed skeptical but made an effort to be supportive anyway. And still others lit up, as if they'd been waiting for us, and vowed to assist in any way they could.

Now that I'm an adult myself—possibly too old to move a piano into a tiny office and wait to see how people react—I try hard to be a cheerleader for today's activists. I can't always manage it, and that makes me appreciate our early encouragers all the more.

Florence Luscomb, who was in her late eighties, sent shivers down our spines when she told us about how her mother had taken her to meet Susan B. Anthony, a leader of the nineteenth-century women's suffrage movement, when she was five years old. Luscomb had grown up to become a suffragist herself and a lifelong activist. She took the microphone at our first outdoor rally in 1974.

Another fervent supporter was the leader of a civil liberties group who wore her hair in an old-fashioned bun. She talked with us about the landmark agreement reached in January 1973 between the US Equal Employment Opportunity Commission and AT&T, then the nation's largest employer, which awarded $45 million in back pay and raises to women and workers of color. (The following year, a second decree would provide

another $30 million. Soon after that, a suit against nine steel produc-
ers would result in $20 million in back pay, and General Electric would
agree to pay out nearly $30 million.) Action by government agencies could
produce important victories, our friend said. But in and of itself, she cau-
tioned, a lawsuit or a charge wasn't enough. In fact, when individuals
called her organization for help with filing a charge, she advised them
just to look for another job. We'd have to find additional ways to press
for fair treatment.

Despite the rapidly changing economy, most scholars seemed to believe
that the true face of labor was male and industrial. But Roslyn Feldberg, a
sociology professor at Boston University, had a different view. She spent
long hours sharing her findings with us, and her lessons were an eye-
opener. We began to understand how office work had become increasingly
important in the economy over the past seventy-five years, and how, in
the process, it had been transformed from a high-paying job for men into
a low-paying job for women.

Until the end of the 1800s, the office clerk and the bookkeeper were
treated like members of the business owner's family. In fact, they often
were members of the family—the owner's sons or sons-in-law. As late as
1900, more than 75 percent of office workers were male, and they earned
twice as much as production and transportation workers.

But then everything changed. With the tremendous growth of industry in the late nineteenth century, the need for administrative services
increased exponentially. Sons and sons-in-law moved up the ladder into
newly created managerial positions, and women—known at first as *typewriters*—were recruited to take their place. Stenography and typing came
to be seen as "women's work." As the work was "feminized," it was seen
as less prestigious. Pay dropped to the bottom of the scale.

As industry expanded, new factory jobs needed filling too. To recruit
workers for these positions, early twentieth-century employers turned
to two demographic groups: American-born farm girls and immigrants
from across the seas. The farm girls were considered temporary workers
who were supplementing the family income until they got married. They

didn't need a living wage, did they? The immigrants, too—male and female alike—were considered worthy of only the lowest pay. They were stereotyped as unreliable, uneducated, and unfit for promotion. Desperately poor, they were forced to settle for subsistence wages.

Now, said Professor Feldberg, let's look at the situation for office workers today. Just like back then, occupational segregation and cultural stereotypes had created a pool of low-paid workers—this time in the modern office. Just like yesterday's "typewriters" and yesterday's factory workers, today's women office workers were seen as less educated, less fit for promotion, and less in need of a decent wage. The rate of job segregation by sex in our era was just as great as in 1900. Eighty percent of women workers occupied low-paying, low-status jobs. Women were 90 percent of bank tellers, 87 percent of file clerks, 90 percent of keypunch operators, 96 percent of receptionists, 97 percent of typists, 99 percent of secretaries. Black and Latina women were beginning to move out of farm and domestic jobs into the office, but their pay and upward mobility lagged. Crammed into low-paying jobs, women of all ages and races were systematically blocked from the higher rungs of the career ladder. Employers could pay low wages to women office workers without fear that they would go elsewhere. They had nowhere to go.

Multiple waves of organizing had turned things around for industrial workers said Professor Feldberg. In the early twentieth century, farm girls and immigrants who worked in the mills and factories had risen up on a massive scale. Then, in the 1930s and '40s, another wave of organizing had improved wages and working conditions for steelworkers, autoworkers, and other industrial workers. Assembly-line workers now earned twice what office workers did. Office work paid less than every category of blue-collar work.

And now, in our own time, a new wave of union organizing was underway. Across the country, public employees were organizing. Until the 1950s, public employees had been largely prohibited by law from unionizing. Now they were making up for lost time. In 1961 President John F. Kennedy had authorized unions for federal employees. States began passing laws that allowed or even encouraged public-sector unions. In 1970, a postal strike swept through New York City and twelve other cities. Firefighters, police officers, and prison guards were organizing.

Teachers were organizing. Inspired in part by the civil rights movement and enabled by the new laws, women working in all levels of government and in hospitals were organizing.

All these newly mobilized workers were gaining higher pay and benefits. Could office workers join in the action? Yes, the professor concluded, indeed we could. Women office workers would be confined to low-paying dead-end jobs only so long as we continued to settle for less. Organizing had not yet turned things around in the office world, but someday it would. Our day was sure to come.

———————

If unionizing was going to be the way forward for office workers, then we 9 to 5'ers needed to reach out and forge a link with the unions in our area. Alas, our first attempts were disappointing, to say the least.

"If I could just get a girl in here to do my typing," a tin-eared union official told us when we showed up in his office, "I'd be out there organizing with you."

There was worse. "Women can't be organized," another official said. "Women think with their cunts, not their brains."

Barbara Fifield of the electrical workers' union was one of the rare female union officials we could find to talk to. She told us that a group of ten clerical workers had recently shown up in her office and expressed interest in joining the union. No one had had any idea what to do with them, and they'd been sent away. But we shouldn't be discouraged, she said. Once we won a union drive, the news would spread. Unions would come running, wanting to join forces.

How could we win a union drive, though? We weren't a union. We barely knew what a union drive entailed. Nonetheless, as we left our lunch with Barbara, we felt not crushed but cheered by the challenge and more convinced than ever that there was a need for what we were aiming to do.

Every few weeks I wrote to Heather, summing up what was happening and asking for advice about what to do next. Just putting my thoughts down on paper was valuable, and knowing someone was listening felt like a gift. Heather's words of encouragement were a special bonus. She had a way of urging me on without providing definite answers. Now I see that she often didn't *have* the answers. But it didn't matter. Her light touch was just what I needed. "Your analysis of your problems is a joy to read," was a typical message from her. Or: "When you ask questions, you seem to answer them yourself." "I just want to reinforce what you imply." "You sound as if you are doing fine. Congratulations."

People like Heather and others who were most helpful seemed to know that every era calls for its own tactics, and that activists of each movement create their own strategies, which may or may not look like those of the previous period. It was strikes and sit-ins for the labor movement of the 1930s and '40s, marches and civil disobedience for the civil rights movement, mass meetings and demonstrations for the antiwar movement, teach-ins and campus shutdowns for the student movement, consciousness-raising circles for the women's movement, and now . . . we at 9 to 5 would be drawing on the wisdom of the past while inventing our own way forward.

Out of the blue, someone knocked on the frosted door of our office and asked if she could join our staff. Janet Selcer had been working at Harvard Business School, where office workers were treated, in her words, "like wallpaper." One time, she passed her boss on the street and he didn't recognize her. Her job, and that of a whole room full of women, was to grade student essays. Knowing next to nothing about the subject matter, they were given a template and told to assign scores. They worked fast, and when the number of papers they were required to handle each hour went up and then up again, Janet circulated a petition. She was called into the personnel office. "You don't seem happy," she was told. "We're going to have to let you go." Now here she was, ready to help make things better for women like her throughout the city.

Since Janet had been fired by the business school, she was entitled to a biweekly unemployment check. Karen was still working part-time at Harvard, so she was getting by too. But I was running through my bank account, and 9 to 5's funds were down to only $375. "Start-up capital" was an expression we'd never heard. All we knew was that we needed cash, and fast. The Y had given us office supplies and a phone line. But each issue of the newsletter cost $220, the rent was $50 a month, my salary was $50 a week, and we still owed the Midwest Academy for part of my tuition. We sent out a hundred fundraising letters to the usual suspects—donors we knew from the antiwar movement—but all we got back was a single check for $100.

I started waking up in the middle of the night choking, unable to breathe.

What could we do? Hold a white elephant sale, someone suggested. A raffle. Pass the hat at meetings—but we weren't even having meetings yet. Start a speakers' bureau. Ask relatives to give us money instead of Christmas presents.

I wrote again to Heather for advice. Try going door-to-door, she suggested. I couldn't imagine it.

Finally, one of our members hit on the idea of approaching the national women's committee of her church. We received a grant of $3,500, which seemed like a fortune. For the time being, we were set.

If we were to stick to the schedule we'd agreed on, we had only a few weeks to come up with a plan of action. Along with Joan Tighe, a member of our group, Karen and I met to prepare a strategy paper for our fellow 9 to 5'ers.

We started out with a couple of paragraphs of economic and cultural context. The time was ripe, we wrote, for what we were aiming to do. As US companies by the thousands were closing factories in the unionized northern states and moving to the South and overseas, another kind of "flight" was also in progress: a massive flight of capital out of the *industrial* sector of the economy into the *service* sector—*our* sector—where, as Professor Feldberg had spelled out, discrimination was helping to keep wages low.

The year we started our organization would turn out to be the great economic tipping point. Beginning in 1973, for the first time since World War II, the average American family began to fare worse than before. Economic hardships that had long been a reality for poor families, especially families of color, now began to affect middle-class families of all races. Families that had gotten by on *one* job now needed *two* wage earners to make ends meet. Men who'd been laid off from high-paying factory jobs were forced to settle for service jobs at half the pay—and their wives needed to work too. The gap between the average worker's pay and the average boss's salary soared.

Along with these economic shifts came sweeping cultural changes. Years of civil rights activism—marches and civil disobedience, sit-ins and boycotts, lawsuits and lobbying—had opened up new opportunities in employment, housing, and education and had heightened expectations of equality and respect throughout society. Growing out of the civil rights movement, the women's movement made people throughout society examine their lives from a new perspective.

As a result of what historian Lane Windham would later call "the coming together of two rivers"—the economic and the cultural—women were joining the workforce in record numbers. Black women had always had a high rate of workforce participation. Now White women were pouring into the workforce. In 1960, 62 percent of families in the United States fit the standard picture of a working father and a stay-at-home mother. Within less than a generation, only 10 percent would. People were marrying later, getting divorced, not marrying at all. In 1970 fewer than a third of women with preschool children worked. Just six years later, 43 percent did.

In the office world, our strategy paper went on, conditions were first rate for combating inequality. Profits were among the highest in any industry, and the office structure was perfect for on-the-job training and upward mobility. Now was the time to awaken women and their employers, unions and government, the media and the public at large, to the realities of working women's lives. And not only to bring those realities into the open, but to change them for the better.

How to go about it? We prepared a list of questions—tough questions—for the group to discuss:

- Should we focus strictly on the office workforce?
- Should we limit ourselves to downtown Boston, or go farther afield?
- Should we focus only on women who wanted action *now*—the vanguard, so to speak—or also try to attract women who weren't yet ready to act?
- Should we strive to be a "pure" group, or welcome a wide range of views? How wide?

- Should we open the group to managers, or limit it to those below the supervisory level?
- Should men be allowed to join?
- Given the class diversity of the office workforce, could we create an organization where both working-class and middle-class women felt comfortable? How?
- How would the lack of racial diversity in the Boston office workforce affect our organizing?
- Were bosses persuadable or outright enemies?
- What about government agencies—friends or enemies?
- Should we promote unionizing? How?

In the weeks and months to come, we took up one question after the other. We followed our intuitions, groped our way ahead. At the time, we couldn't see the shape of the new form we were about to create—or how powerful it would be. But if we weren't exactly sure how to improve the lives of office workers, no one else seemed to know either, so we figured we might as well get on with it.

We estimated that from start to finish (whatever "finish" might mean—unionizing by the millions?), the whole project would take about five years. Don't ask how we came up with that number.

4

"I'M NOT A FEMINIST, BUT . . ."

ALL THROUGH SEPTEMBER, calls came in on the phone line the Y had given us, first a trickle, then more. We set out to meet these callers, along with the women who'd written to us in response to the newsletter over the past year. Soon enough, we hoped to take on the corporate titans of Boston and make them change their ways. But first—there was no way around it—the crucial groundwork had to be laid. We had to eat a lot of lunches.

As I'd learned in Chicago, step one was to dress like the women we hoped to recruit. I'd left my red-white-and-blue skirt and top behind in Chicago; I couldn't bear to bring them home. We studied the apparel of the women our age streaming into the office towers. Flimsy little pastel tops, slim slacks, short tan raincoats. Joan gave us a lesson on accessories— scarves, delicate gold necklaces. All very femme. We couldn't really get the hang of it. I remember a yellow crocheted vest that I wore a lot in those days, which I thought was sort of dressy; today it's obvious to me that no one else in the office workforce was wearing anything remotely like it. Karen favored shapeless shirts. Janet's favorite outfit was a short faux fur jacket paired with big round-toed suede shoes.

We kept trying. I went to Filene's Basement, a place the size of a football field where you took off your clothes in the aisles to try things on, and acquired a pants-skirt-jacket-vest set made of dark brown wool. It was unbelievably ugly, but I wore it whenever I could stand to. I couldn't bring myself to follow Heather's advice about carrying a lipstick in my purse, much less using it. A short, tidy haircut was about as far as I could go. I still mourned my mop of red curls.

Dressed in our bizarre costumes, we plunged into the fray. Every morning around eleven o'clock, we'd set out across the Public Garden with its swan boats and hurry through the Boston Common. We ate lunch after lunch—sometimes three a day—at little corner restaurants thronged with downtown workers. As recommended by my teachers at the Midwest Academy, we'd order coffee and a small sandwich. We usually skipped the pie they'd also suggested. Once in a while we met people after work, but not often. Karen came back reeling from a happy hour with some legal secretaries. When they all ordered White Russians, she did too, but soon realized she'd made a terrible mistake.

At each meal, we followed the script I'd received in my training. The heart of every encounter was listening:

Why did you get in touch with 9 to 5?
Do you like your job?
Does your boss treat you with respect?
Have you ever felt discriminated against?
What kinds of jobs do women hold in your office?
Do men do the same work? Do they get paid the same?
What are your coworkers most concerned about?

The closing was just as important: "It certainly sounds as if something needs to be done at your company. But it's hard to change policies as an individual. Let me tell you about 9 to 5."

The goal, as Steve had stressed at the Midwest Academy, was not just a nice chat but a commitment. At this point, it wasn't easy to come up with what a commitment might be. So far, we didn't have a lot of ways for people to be involved. "Can you help distribute the newsletter before work?" "Can you think of other women you can talk to about 9 to 5?" These were the early assignments we created for women new to our cause. Later, we would develop many more.

All of this might seem obvious, but it wasn't to me. Sitting across the table from a woman I didn't know felt like being on a date. Awkward!

It was hard for me to keep the conversation on track. I learned a lot of irrelevant information about people's boyfriends and husbands, and even their pets, before I mastered how to direct the conversation. And on occasions when I was foolish enough to deviate from the recommended coffee and sandwich, I suffered a series of food mishaps—a cherry tomato skittering across the table, an incident with an artichoke. Eventually, though, I got these meetings down to a formula, and they began to seem easy.

After our lunches, we rushed back to the office to record what had happened in our collective notebook. A lot of what we were seeing and hearing was a surprise.

We thought that most of the women who wanted to meet with us would call themselves feminists. Not so. "I believe women should be treated equally on the job," we heard over and over. "But I am *not* a feminist. *Not* a women's libber." As the historian Linda Gordon has written in *Feminism Unfinished: A Short, Surprising History of American Women's Movements*, the women's liberation movement that was flowering across America was the largest social movement in US history. But that didn't mean the women we were meeting wanted to embrace the label.

Maybe because of our own cluelessness when it came to clothing, we'd expected that the least well-dressed women would be most inclined to join. That was dead wrong. Those who were most interested tended to dress impeccably.

We expected to hear a lot of complaints about boredom. But we didn't hear much along those lines. It was the women most deeply invested in their jobs and their companies who cared about making things better. This letter from a legal secretary was typical:

> I do my job extremely well. I believe I am good enough at my work and my job is important enough that I deserve to be paid enough to go home at night without worrying about my utility bills, drive a decent car, live in a decent house, and be able to afford to see a movie once in a while. I do not think red meat should be a luxury in my house. I think my daughter and I should receive adequate medical care. I do not think this is too much to ask.

Or this one, more formally phrased:

> I am caught in the ambivalence of feeling, on the one hand, deep
> personal involvement in my work and in the goals of the company
> and, on the other hand, ever-growing frustration arising from the
> knowledge that my employer will never accord me the recogni-
> tion I deserve, either through pay or through promotions. I'd like
> to make some changes but don't know how, and would deeply
> appreciate the assistance of a knowledgeable and supportive group.

We thought women our age—young women—would be most likely
to join, and this was true. But it wasn't uncommon for older women to
say that they'd been waiting for years for something like 9 to 5 to come
along. One day a woman in her fifties came swirling into the office. I
seem to remember—could this be?—that she was wearing some kind of
medieval-looking cape. "You are brave warriors!" she cried.

Day after day, in our beehive of an office, we talked and talked about
what we'd heard over our coffee and sandwiches. Women were telling us
that they felt unrecognized and disrespected. Some told us they did the
same work as men for less. Some worked outside their job descriptions
(if they had job descriptions) for no extra pay. Many were expected to do
favors—all kinds of favors—for their bosses. A college education didn't
necessarily translate into a better job, and neither did years of experience.
Even though the practice of listing men's and women's jobs in different
columns in the newspaper—HELP WANTED MALE and HELP WANTED
FEMALE—was at an end (nudged along by picket lines and lawsuits), most
women were still hired into "women's" jobs, and they remained in "wom-
en's" jobs year after year. Time and again, we heard about young White
men being promoted over women with years of skills and experience.

Back then, no one used the term "glass ceiling"—meaning that women
could advance only so high before bumping up against a sometimes invisible limit. But the phenomenon was real. We heard about a woman at a
large Boston bank who asked to be reimbursed for an economics course
and was turned down on the grounds that the class was not job related.
Six months later, a man was reimbursed for a course in English literature.
He rose up the career ladder; she stayed where she was.

"I have found clerical work to be a direct stepping stone to more clerical work," a woman wrote us, "especially if you are good at it."

"In the fifteen years I've been in my department," said another, "I've trained three department managers." Her boss told her that she did her job so well he couldn't afford to promote her. Instead, he brought in young, White men from outside the company, and she was the one who had to train them.

An article that had recently been published in *New York* magazine confirmed her point: Men "generally begin their careers at exactly the point most young women have been trying to reach for years," the author wrote. "Men don't have to begin as secretaries and survive the long period of initiation in which a woman is valued not just for what she does, but for those negative qualities that her role so often requires: lack of independent judgment, absence of initiative, fear of displaying ambition."

A woman in her sixties told us she hated it when her boss, who was many years her junior, referred to her as "my girl." "We are referred to as girls," another woman wrote in, "until the day we retire without pension."

Women told us how annoyed they were that the office hierarchy seemed designed to replicate women's role as domestic helpmeets. "If they're not treating you like a machine," one woman wrote us, "they act as if you're their personal servant, existing solely to cater to them."

Sometimes, the irritants were little things. "A guy will be practically sitting in the Xerox room," a woman complained, "and he'll call me over from the other end of the office to ask me to make one copy." Just like my boss, the one who walked all the way down the hall to ask me to remove the calendar from his wall.

Other times, it was big things that got under women's skin. "One of the reasons I wanted to work at the university was to meet students and professors," a woman said. "But I'm on a different social level here. Secretaries aren't supposed to understand the men's papers—they're just supposed to type them."

Many women were happy with secretarial work itself but dismayed by how others perceived the job. "The most crushing thing," a university office worker said, "is when you're with a group of students or teachers and somebody asks what you do." Tell them you're a secretary, she said, and watch them turn away.

In the newsletter, we printed a provocative list of questions drawn up by a New York office worker:

Is your job considered a woman's job? Why?

Do you receive the benefits that many unionized women enjoy (pensions, regular increases, seniority protection, maternity leave)?

Could your office function if the office workers went on strike?

Are you treated as a human being, or as an extension of your typewriter, switchboard, or filing cabinet?

Does your boss ever forget your name? Do you ever forget his?

Do you order your boss's lunch, buy presents for his kids, sharpen his pencils?

Does he do these things for you?

Does your boss blame his errors on you? Does he take credit for your good ideas?

Almost all the women we saw entering the office towers in the morning were White, as was our original core group—and the Boston workforce as a whole. (In the 1970s, more than 90 percent of the Boston area workforce was White; by 2019 that figure was 84 percent.) The office workforce in particular was largely closed to non-White employees. Only 4 percent of Boston-area office workers were non-White in 1973, a figure that had increased to 10 percent by 2019.

The cleaning shifts, after 5:00 PM, were a different story. That was when women of color reported for work in the big downtown buildings. And farther out of town, we discovered several large data processing centers where Black women worked in low-paid clerical jobs. One reason we would eventually go national was to build a multiracial organization. In Baltimore, Cleveland, Atlanta, and other cities with significant numbers of non-White office workers, we devoted ourselves—successfully—to building organizations as racially diverse as the workforce itself.

Boston's clerical workforce was remarkably diverse when it came to class. The concept of class as we experienced it was slippery, though. Typical of the United States as a whole, everyone in the office world was aware of class differences, but talking explicitly about them was pretty much taboo. The term "working class" was rarely heard. Most people described themselves as middle class, even those whom economists would assign to a lower or higher bracket.

At the Midwest Academy, Steve had suggested that we think of two classes: owners and nonowners. Owners give orders; nonowners take orders. Owners decide what others do and what they themselves do; nonowners depend on their jobs as their only form of support. No one ever used those terms out loud either. Nonetheless, markers of class were everywhere—in how people spoke, how they dressed, where they'd grown up and where they lived now, what they aspired to and where their sympathies lay.

We met many women who came from the area's famous White ethnic neighborhoods, the ones lined with wooden three-deckers, where most of the workers, especially men, held factory jobs. For women in these communities, an office job was a step up. Dressing up, working in a clean, quiet place, and having your own desk were emblems of rising up in the world. What could be disappointing—indeed, shocking—was the pay. As the ideas of the women's movement spread throughout society, women in this category were as annoyed as anyone else about the disrespect they experienced.

Another large group we met had never aspired to end up behind a typewriter. They'd earned college degrees and tended to live in the hipper areas clustered around college campuses, or in neighborhoods farther from downtown. With their college educations, many had expected to work at professional jobs in the downtown businesses. Instead, they found themselves at the bottom of the ladder and could see no way up. Some, like me, were recent graduates. Others, in the absurd parlance of the time, were known as "displaced homemakers"—women in their thirties and older who were thought to be in the work world solely as a result of an unfortunate accident, like divorce, widowhood, or a husband's layoff. Many in this category were angry to find themselves treated like nothing more than a set of ten typing fingers.

So we found women from all across the class spectrum sitting side by side. Class differences could be a cause of friction and distrust. But to an increasing extent, office workers looked around at one another and felt united—as women.

As we listened to how our lunchmates spoke, we learned to avoid certain words and substitute others. *Wages* became *pay* or *salary. Workers* were *employees. Boss* became *employer* or *management. Discrimination* was not a word we often heard, though that was changing. No one ever used the word *organize*. At this point, we rarely spoke the word *union* either, as it made people fear being fired, and reasonably so.

Why risk having our words get in the way of our ideas? Karl Marx stirringly exhorted: "Workers of the world, unite; you have nothing to lose but your chains!" If that famous appeal were translated into office workerese, we joked, it might sound something like this: "We're getting together in the cafeteria next Tuesday. Can you make it?"

Along with our vocabulary, we were also honing our core principles. The unwritten manifesto we were developing, which owed something to the Midwest Academy's three-part mantra, went like this:

- Office work and office workers deserve respect. The point is not to move everyone out of office jobs, but to improve pay, working conditions, and opportunity in those jobs.
- Employers are mistreating women and breaking the law. Management—not the government—is the target.
- To make change, women need to join together.

These principles distinguished us from others in the women's movement who were more likely to call clerical jobs demeaning and focus on helping women to get out of them. Nor were we about training individual employees to try to make it on their own, though in fact countless individual women *did* get promoted thanks to 9 to 5. We were about fanning the flames of discontent and helping women to improve their work lives through collective action.

We felt different from the social scientists and union officials who put the focus on the failings of women themselves. If women office workers were underpaid and unorganized, these people claimed, maybe it was because they were loyal to their bosses or even in love with them. Women didn't trust one another. They thought they were too good for unions. They lacked self-confidence. They'd internalized the image of the secretary: ninny, sex object, surrogate wife. And on and on.

Yes, yes, yes. Any of these things might have been true to one extent or another. But we didn't want to talk about what was wrong with women. Employers, not employees, were the problem. Company policies were the problem. That's what we wanted to talk about.

We were different, too, from the "fair employment consultants" hired by companies to run career training sessions. *Anyone* can make it, was these consultants' message. ("Lean in" was the advice aimed at women half a century later.) But not *everyone*, we pointed out. Yes, we wanted career ladders, but let's also improve life in the typing pool—the "pink-collar ghetto"—itself.

An office worker who was trying to organize a union in New York put it like this: "For everyone who makes it, there will be countless others who won't, unless we start doing what other workers have done"—joining together. "They may offer you a promotion to shut you up," she continued. "Take the promotion and keep on organizing."

———————

After spending many weeks listening and talking over what we'd learned, with great excitement we began to prepare for our first public meeting. We kept three points in mind:

- Keep it short.
- Leave nothing to chance.
- Present a plan for action.

Our debut event would be like the trick flowers I used to love as a girl—bits of folded paper that would bloom into larger versions of themselves when you immersed them in a glass of water. We vowed that our lineup of speakers would resemble the workforce as a whole: old, young, middle class, working class, White, Black. At every stage, even at our smallest, we wanted our organization to look like the population we represented. We'd aim to bring in the greatest number, welcoming the hesitant as well as those who were already with us. We'd seek to set a clear direction and start moving forward. Hop on, ladies!

Our speakers would stand at a podium and lay out the problems they were experiencing. We'd offer information about legal rights. And we'd present our action plan for demanding changes in company policies.

What the meeting would *not* be was a discussion circle, as was common at the beginning of the women's movement and as our group had started out. It would not be a place where women would raise their hands and express their thoughts. Not, as had been common in the student movement, a room full of people deciding on the spot what to do next. These formats had served their purpose in their time, but now we were up to something different.

We drew up a leaflet announcing a "Forum for Women Office Workers" to be held on a Monday from 5:30 to 7:00 PM at the Y. One of our new contacts who worked in a graphic design firm supplied a sketch of a modern-looking typewriter with a sheet of paper scrolling out of the roller. "It's time we took a good look at our situation and started doing something about it," said the message, in typewriter font. Three questions followed:

- What are the problems we share?
- What are our rights under the law?
- What can we do to help ourselves?

Everything about the leaflet was as mild as could be, from the pale pink of the paper, to the delicately drawn graphic, to the politely worded text. We handed out fifteen thousand copies all over town, and we ran fifteen- and thirty-second spots—free "public service announcements"—on radio stations.

But just putting out the word was only the beginning. The nitty-gritty was dividing up our list of names and making phone call after phone call. Each contact had her own index card where we recorded the date she was called, how she responded, how likely she was to attend, and how many people she could bring with her, if any. Those who said yes got a second reminder call.

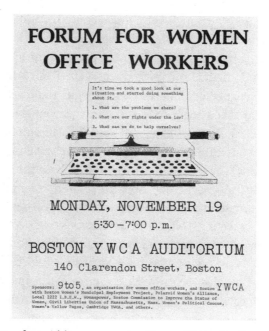

FORUM FOR WOMEN OFFICE WORKERS

It's time we took a good look at our situation and started doing something about it.

1. What are the problems we share?

2. What are our rights under the law?

3. What can we do to help ourselves?

MONDAY, NOVEMBER 19
5:30 – 7:00 p.m.

BOSTON YWCA AUDITORIUM
140 Clarendon Street, Boston

Sponsors: 9 to 5, an organization for women office workers, and Boston YWCA with Boston Women's Municipal Employment Project, Polaroid Women's Alliance, Local 2222 I.B.E.W., Womanpower, Boston Commission to Improve the Status of Women, Civil Liberties Union of Massachusetts, Mass. Women's Political Caucus, Women's Yellow Pages, Cambridge YWCA, and others.

Our first public event was a "forum." We distributed thousands of pink flyers. *Author's collection*

As a teenager, I'd been afraid of making phone calls. I even had to write out a script to call up a movie theater:

Me: Hello. What time is the show?
[Space for answer]
Me: Thank you.

Now, I screwed up my courage and just did it. Somehow, as I read the words off my script in call after call, I felt more and more at ease. It wasn't so bad.

———————

A month after Jeff's father died, I'd gone down to Baltimore for the memorial service. Away from the intensity of my new life, I read through the pile of condolence letters and at last found myself able to feel for Jeff's family and to cry. His mother, through her own tears, looked at the two of us and made a sweet remark: "You make him happy."

Now Jeff was back in Boston. When I picked him up at the airport, he looked sad and fragile, and now once again I felt torn between the demands of my new persona and those of my girlfriend self. In the weeks to come, when he asked for a hug, sometimes I was glad to oblige, but other times, after a long day at the Y, I wasn't in the mood. Should I do it anyway? Or pay attention to what *I* wanted? He wasn't always there for me when *I* felt low, was he? So was it my job to help him out every time he needed me? Such were the questions I explored at length in my diary.

Jeff was an unfailingly excellent sounding board—endlessly curious about who I was meeting, what office workers were saying, what I was thinking. He learned everyone's names, bragged about 9 to 5 to everyone he knew, and told me how much he wished he could be part of something like it. Like me, he was moving away from the antiwar movement style of organizing, with its unruly public meetings. After years in the student movement, he'd taken his job at the hospital not only to earn a salary but also to do something "real." Now—and with my certificate from the Midwest Academy to prove it—I was demonstrating that being an organizer was real.

Real, yes. Easy, no. The night before our forum I was weeping in bed, convinced that the next evening we were destined for failure. Jeff sat down next to me and we held on to each other. Maybe we could love each other, whatever that meant. And maybe the forum would turn out all right.

The next evening, November 19, 1973, the entrance to the Y was bustling. As women streamed into the building, representatives of half a dozen socialist organizations lined the sidewalk, brandishing leaflets and newspapers. We were not surprised. It was in part because of them that our meeting included no time for discussion. If we'd opened the floor, they would have stood up to assert—in words far outside of our carefully constructed lexicon—that our fledgling organization should declare its support for X or oppose Y. And if that happened, we feared, the women we were aiming to involve would be puzzled at best and maybe turned off for good.

As I'd learned at the Midwest Academy, we set up fewer chairs than we thought we'd need, so if we had to go get more, everyone would see that the event had turned out to be bigger than expected. And it was! Thrillingly, office workers kept coming: 120, 150. We even spotted a newspaper reporter in their midst.

The education director of the Y opened the meeting, and then Lillian Christmas, a legal secretary, one of the rare Black women in the office workforce, gave a talk she titled "Speaking from Experience." "After nearly a quarter century, why does my employer have so little respect for my skills and abilities?" she asked. "Why is my salary so low that I have to take in freelance typing to support my family?" She found it insulting, too, that her boss rarely referred to her by her name, but instead used terms like "the girl," "the kid," "sunshine," or "honey child."

Donna Mathews, from our original group of ten, spoke next. She'd grown up looking forward to working in an office, she said, but found her job deeply disappointing—dead-end and poorly paid. She felt taken for granted. "If someone wants something Xeroxed or something from downstairs, I'm always the one who gets interrupted." Like so many others, she'd trained a man to advance over her.

The lawyer who shared our office outlined the legal rights that could be used by individuals and groups alike. Thanks to the civil rights movement, we had antidiscrimination laws at the federal, state, and local levels. Thanks to the union movement, we had labor laws. These could be powerful tools, but we would have to use them in combination with other forms of power. Our rights, she stressed, would not be handed to us.

Karen finished off the program with our plan of action. Our first step would be to document the facts about office work and office workers in Boston, both by gathering statistics and by asking office workers all over town to share their stories. At this point we brought out big stacks of a survey form that asked women to tell us about pay and benefits, overtime, promotion opportunities, job training, job descriptions, personal errands for the boss, and discrimination—with plenty of space for comments. We needed everyone to help distribute the survey, Karen said, and in ten days' time we'd meet again to move forward with presenting the results to employers, public officials, and the public at large.

We'd start, she said, by asking the Chamber of Commerce to hear our case. This body was one of the few corporate entities in the office world that presented a public face. Mostly, employers kept their human resources operations safely hidden behind the shiny windows of their soaring buildings. The chamber, on the other hand, existed specifically to further communication between the business community and the outside world. Well, we had some things to communicate.

With that, the meeting was adjourned. It had lasted barely half an hour—much shorter than we'd expected. But the room was abuzz. People stayed around to talk, and the table piled with surveys was mobbed as women picked up armloads to distribute.

HUB WOMEN OFFICE WORKERS UNITE FOR HIGHER PAY, read the headline in the *Boston Globe* the next day. OVERWORKED, UNDERPAID AND UNDERVALUED. We were in the news!

We were exhausted. We were thrilled. We had done it. We were launched.

5

A BILL OF RIGHTS FOR
WOMEN OFFICE WORKERS

Up to that time, office employers had not been much challenged by their underlings, but as working women began to awaken, undoubtedly their bosses, too, would begin to stir. What would they do? Would they give in? Or fight back? It was time to find out.

In keeping with the dictum that every meeting had to have a purpose, our first gathering after the forum was devoted to planning our upcoming appointment with the Chamber of Commerce—specifically, with a certain Mr. K., who headed the chamber's personnel managers' group. The idea was to swoop into Mr. K.'s office at lunchtime and demand that he attend a "hearing" about women office workers to be held a couple of months later. At the hearing, women would speak out about their problems and demand change.

Thanks to our concerted phone calling, some fifty women showed up for the planning meeting. Once again, we had to set up more chairs. Joan ran the program. Dressed for the occasion in a matching top and skirt with tasteful accessories, she looked and sounded as if she were perfectly comfortable in the role, but in fact it was her first time ever behind a podium.

Joan wasn't the only one doing something new. Many in the room, we suspected, had never been to a meeting of any kind before. There were nervous giggles, as well as supportive bursts of applause, as we all introduced ourselves. And there were chuckles as we passed out our new 9 to 5 song, written by Jan Levine (now Jan Levine Thal) to the tune of "Charlie on the MTA," the Boston anthem everyone knew:

> Let me tell you the story of a woman named Susie
> who applied for a job one day.
> They tested her for typing, for shorthand and speedwriting,
> then they gave her the lowest pay.
>
> (Refrain:)
> We type and file 9 to 5
> Yet we barely stay alive
> Working from day to day.
> Well, we've done a day's work in the offices of Boston
> And it's time we got a day's pay!

There were several more verses, and we sang them all—twice.

A few dozen women agreed to come to the lunchtime showdown with Mr. K. Amazingly, he didn't cancel. I served as the spokeswoman—a first for me, and as far as I can remember, the last. (From that point on, women working in offices would take the public roles.) I read out a long, florid set of remarks (perhaps too long and perhaps too florid) charging that "the Chamber of Commerce bears responsibility for intolerable, illegal, and unfair employment policies."

Mr. K. was incredulous. *Illegal? Unfair? How could we think such a thing?*

We see it every day, we said.

He raised an eyebrow. "Show me the evidence," he said, "and I'll get back to you." Upon which he and his associates rose from their chairs, bringing the meeting to a close.

A few days later we received a cordial letter from Mr. K. "The exchange of views was beneficial to all concerned," he wrote. "We will await receipt of the information we requested and will review it carefully with an eye toward assisting you—if at all possible."

In the bowels of the Federal Building, several of us pored over thick books stuffed with statistics. We had no trouble coming up with a long list of damning figures. But by the time we sent them to Mr. K., the chamber had changed direction. "I thank you," Mr. K.'s next and final letter read, "for sending me the material on the 9 to 5 organization and also the statistics which you have collected."

He went on:

> We here at the Greater Boston Chamber of Commerce have given a great deal of thought as to how we might cooperate with your group. We have come to the firm conclusion that the program you have in mind relative to employment of women office workers cannot and does not fit into activities of the Chamber.
>
> Salaries and conditions of work are the responsibilities of individual firms. The charter of the Chamber does not permit it to inject itself into matters of an intimate nature such as personnel policies and wages. I would respectfully suggest that individual members of 9 to 5 who feel they have legitimate complaints arrange to discuss such matters with the particular employers concerned.

At the very bottom of the letter, as was the custom, Mr. K.'s initials appeared in uppercase letters, followed by the lowercase initials of the secretary who'd typed the letter, like this: JGK:eb.

Who was "eb," we wondered, and what was she thinking as she typed the letter?

We never heard from the chamber again. But in the months and years to come, as we pursued "matters of an intimate nature such as personnel policies and wages" all over town, women like "eb" would turn out to be a rich source of information.

The chamber's refusal to engage unnerved us. Our attempt to "get into the arena and stay in," as the Midwest Academy urged, had been thwarted.

I wrote to Heather to make sure we were on the right track.

She wrote right back. "Why *would* Mr. K. give in," she probed gently, "other than that you want him to and need a victory?" To my surprise, though, she didn't scold. If the chamber wouldn't come to the table, find something else to do, she urged. Make sure it's something your members feel comfortable with.

And so we left the chamber behind and went ahead with plans for a "Hearing on the Working Conditions of Women Office Workers" in April, three months hence, where we'd present the statistics we'd dug up at Mr. K.'s request along with "testimony" about women's problems in the office. The audience would consist of as many office workers, public officials, and employers as we could persuade to show up.

Now we had to find women to speak at the hearing, invite the public officials, try to rustle up some employers, make sure we got covered in the media—and fill the hall. Back to the lunch circuit. Women were amazed that after they mailed in a survey, someone cared enough to call them back and schedule a time to get together to hear more. Many were used to being alone with their problems, sometimes feeling abnormal or inadequate because they weren't happy in their jobs, tending to blame themselves for their low pay and lack of advancement opportunity. *I should have gotten that degree,* they lamented. *I should present myself more professionally.* Our message to them was that the problem was not their individual shortcomings but an unfair system of employment, and that the solution was to band together. For many, this was an eye-opener.

The phone kept ringing, survey returns kept coming, and everything we heard was entered into our collective notebook. We started to hear tales of insurrection, or stirrings in that direction, anyway.

Women in a small office banded together and agreed that the next day they'd all wear striped blouses to convey the idea that their workplace was like a prison.

At Harvard a group of women wrote a memo demanding that professors answer their own phones, type their own personal letters, and do some of the filing, thus freeing the secretaries to do more interesting work and develop their talents. The director of the department called an all-day meeting to discuss the issues—and gave everyone a $1,000 raise. The women weren't satisfied. The boss hadn't really listened to what they were saying, they felt. The problem wasn't the money. It was that they didn't feel they were treated like full human beings, with full respect.

On a warehouse-sized floor in a giant insurance company, a call came in on the supervisor's phone for Pearl, a woman in her fifties who was raising her grandchildren. "Family emergency," said the caller. "Sorry," said the supervisor. "Pearl is working. She can't come to the phone." Pearl exploded. Outrage spread from pod to pod. Work stopped for the rest of the day, and men—managers from the top offices—appeared on the floor for the first time to break up the conflagration.

At a huge tech company in Cambridge, women demanded that the health insurance plan be changed to cover obstetrical expenses for single as well as married women. To their amazement, management not only agreed right away but also created a job for one of them, Susan, to work on rooting out discrimination. When a problem arose, they were told, all they needed to do was call Susan, and she would put things right. Now what should they do?

Women at the Massachusetts Institute of Technology, the science university that was the very picture of a male-dominated work environment, started holding meetings, and in no time they drew up a list of demands: a formal wage and promotion schedule, longer vacations, a grievance procedure. Soon they planned to present it to management.

Most intriguing of all, we heard about two women working at a tiny insurance agency who summoned the courage to circulate a petition. They wanted higher pay and a long list of other improvements. After three days, their boss caught them at it. He held the petition up in the air and got everyone's attention. "Do you know what we do with these things?" he demanded. "They go straight in the trash." Plunk.

A week later, all the women's demands were met.

All this unrest made us more convinced than ever that change was coming. But although we occasionally ran across a woman who'd been involved in a union organizing effort, we never learned of a successful one. Within the private sector, we didn't encounter a single unionized office. From time to time we'd hear that an employer was trying to blunt our credibility by claiming that 9 to 5 was secretly funded by a union. We weren't. So far, we weren't engaged in any kind of union activity.

We were certainly thinking about it, though. Through binding contracts, many kinds of workers were improving their lot. We felt sure that
office workers, too, would soon turn to unions. A great new surge of
organizing was coming. It was only a matter of time.

But the time had not yet arrived. So at first we didn't actively promote
unionizing. We simply *predicted* that *some* women *would* unionize in the
years to come. At that point, we saw ourselves, among other things, as
intermediaries who could help unions connect to women and help women
connect to unions.

Meanwhile, calls came in regularly from office workers who'd been
fired. "What should I do?" they asked. "Don't they have to give me a
reason? Aren't I entitled to two weeks' notice?"

Unfortunately, the answer was no.

Maybe it was unfair, and yes, they were right to be angry, but unless
they had a union contract or some kind of written agreement, being
fired was not illegal. Women who could prove they'd been fired because
of their race, sex, or age could try their luck with the antidiscrimination agencies, but those agencies were so overloaded that it might not
be worth it. Women who'd been fired specifically for organizing were
protected by the National Labor Relations Act, which covered not just
a union drive but any form of "concerted" activity—meaning any on-
the-job action involving more than one person, including being active
in 9 to 5. The trouble was that it took forever to get a ruling, and in the
meantime, the fired worker was out the door and the organizing effort
tended to fizzle.

These calls were painful to answer. There were no easy solutions, no
individual fixes for systemic issues.

I met with four women from a medium-sized office, one of whom
had just been fired and forced to sign a statement saying she was incom-
petent. They asked us to put them in touch with a union, and we set
up a meeting for them with an organizer from a New York union that
had made noises about coming to Boston. We expected him to try to
sell the women on joining his organization, but he didn't. Instead, he
leaned back in his chair, cigarillo in hand, and warned that forming
a union would be a long, hard process. He didn't offer to help in any
way. Come back when you have at least one good contact in every

department, he said. We never heard from the women again, and I'm sure he didn't either.

Around that time, a veteran union organizer named Frank Lyons, who'd become a labor educator at a local college, took an interest in us. Across the sticky table of a downtown bar, he asked what we were planning to do if and when the women of 9 to 5 became ready for the next step.

"Well," we said, "we'll call up a union and introduce them." Just as we'd done with those four women.

"You mean you'll do all that work," he sputtered, "and then give away your members to someone else? Fools!" We should start our own union, he said.

In the meantime, as the day of our "hearing" drew near, everything felt fresh and exciting. Hurrying to my post-leafleting breakfast at Ken's with Karen and Janet, I walked fast, with big steps, wearing the new teal blue coat I'd bought in the chaos of Filene's Basement. Every morning, before we got down to business figuring out new ways to make trouble, the three of us would spend a few minutes describing our dreams—the ones we'd had while sleeping, that is, not our visions of a better future. We all remembered our dreams in detail, and the morning Janet and I reported we'd had the *same* dream, we were only slightly surprised. We were that tight.

We were making history, Karen told us as we ate our eggs and toast. In Karen's presence, I believed that whatever we were doing mattered deeply. Janet felt the same way.

Ever since Karen and I had met across the freshman seminar table in college, she'd intimidated me, and that, of course, was part of her appeal. Bold, independent, self-motivated, she made me feel I could be the same way. Being in her orbit was both a challenge and a shelter. In the manner of many followers vis-à-vis leaders, I measured myself against her, pretended to be like her, resented her when I fell short of the standard she set. I wanted to be close, I wanted to get away. I wanted to be like her, I wanted to be different. I wanted to use her as a model, I wanted to be my own person. Our relationship was warm and close, but I was a demanding friend, just as I was a demanding girlfriend for Jeff. At times she must have found me exhausting.

Despite these complications, the time we all spent together in the office was great fun—nurturing and collective. I did my best thinking during our discussions and often surprised myself with the insights I heard coming out of my mouth. Yet what we were attempting to do was huge, and as winter deepened, we began to wonder if we were up to it.

One morning I came in from an hour of handing out job surveys in the freezing wind, slammed my bag down on the desk, and announced that I couldn't stand it anymore. Janet confided that she was feeling down-hearted too. She confessed that at a lunch a few days before, she'd popped open a can of diet soda and accidentally sprayed the contents into the face of a prospective member, who then declined to have anything to do with our organization.

We were working about as hard as we could. Long, long days, thirteen hours at a stretch. I poured out my troubles in a letter to my mother. Like Heather, she, too, knew what to say. "My very dear Ellen," she wrote back, "Your letter of frustration was the greatest restorative to my soul that I have had all week."

I felt consoled by her matter-of-fact reaction to my tale of woe, and doubly consoled when she announced she was coming up to Boston for the weekend. When she arrived, I was so overloaded that I took her to the office to help stuff envelopes.

Apart from our recruitment lunches, we barely had time to eat. Sometimes at five thirty I'd stop by a shop on Boylston Street to buy a pretzel stick, a hunk of cheese, and a banana or a Red Delicious apple to tide me over through the dinner hour. Janet brought in bags of carrots and celery to munch on as she made calls, holding the phone receiver away from her mouth to mute the crunching.

In the evenings, the windows were black as we stayed late to reach people on their home phone numbers. We'd attack our stack of index cards with a vengeance, dialing, coaxing, cajoling, convincing. We didn't leave the office till 8:30 or 9:00 PM.

Even the typing was hard. Karen and I were terrible typists. When Karen worked at Harvard, she was given a stack of preprinted letters and a list of doctoral students and told to type in the names, addresses, and salutation (Dear ____). The day after she delivered them to her boss, he handed them back with big red circles around the typos—"Raod" for "Road," "Cmabrgde" for "Cambridge." Karen argued that it didn't really matter because the students all knew how to spell their names and addresses, so what was the big deal? (Amazingly, she kept her job.)

Now, as we churned out newsletters, agendas, leaflets, reports, and letters of invitation, our secretarial skills, or lack thereof, were on full display. When you made a mistake on any of our three manual typewriters or our one state-of-the-art IBM Selectric, you had two choices: you could use correction tape, which would cover the error (sort of) with a flaky powder, or you could paint correction fluid onto the document with a little brush, then wait for the wet patch to dry while blowing on it and inhaling the fumes (toxic, we learned). If you didn't wait long enough (you never did), the patch would smear. For documents requiring multiples, a Gestetner duplicating machine was stationed in the hall. You'd type your text on a waxed stencil, scratching out errors with a paper clip, then slip the sheet into the machine, pour in a batch of strong-smelling ink, and turn the drum by hand, hoping for a minimum of splotches.

All of this was a powerful incentive to get our new members involved. They were *real* secretaries. They knew how to do these things.

Since coming home from Chicago, I'd dropped most of my friends. Some of them had chipped in ten or twenty-five dollars to help pay for my training, and I was grateful, but after reporting in on my summer, I'd pulled away. Many of them were critical of 9 to 5. Instead of just focusing on job problems, they thought we should be spelling out an explicit analysis of the US economy, complete with words like *exploitation, surplus value*, and *capitalist class*.

I shared their views on the economy, and a few months earlier I might have been swayed by their critique. But now I had changed. Now I believed that my job was to seek out the edge of the possible, to get people involved in trying to win something concrete. If there was a "line" we were preaching to our prospective members, it went like this: "You've got problems on the job, and they're probably related to your being a woman. Your boss benefits from all of this. If we want to make things better, we need to do it together." To my old friends, this message seemed far too elementary, but to the women we were meeting, it was a lot to bite off.

One evening I went to a women's poetry reading in a Cambridge church basement. The place was packed. Words like *oppression* and *imperialism* flew through the air. Although the poems spoke to me, I didn't stay long. The event would have made most of our members uncomfortable, and at this point I didn't feel right being there either.

When I was about to leave Chicago, I'd mailed back the tube of revolutionary posters Jeff had sent me so that I wouldn't have to carry it on the plane. The posters disappeared in transit and were never seen again. I didn't miss them.

One frigid Saturday morning I woke up in a panic of loneliness. Jeff was in Baltimore with his mother. My housemates weren't around, and I decided for some reason to head for the ice rink on Somerville Avenue. It was a long, cold walk. Once there I laced up a pair of skates and made my way again and again around the frozen oval. Every circuit felt more pointless than the one before.

On my way back, I remembered that a member of the 9 to 5 core group who worked at the Prudential Insurance Company lived nearby. I rang the bell at her apartment, and when she buzzed me in, I found her sitting in bed next to her boyfriend. Aside from the bed, there was nothing in the room except a dog—and piles of dog shit. The sight of the two (three?) of them—apparently even worse off than I was—only drove me into greater despair.

Shortly after signing the papers for the office at the Y, I'd moved out of Jeff's house into a group house nearby, a gorgeous Victorian that I shared with eight housemates—an economist, a teacher, a nurse, a carpenter, a grad student, and three law students. I loved my room under the eaves with its varnished floor and gleaming white walls and the bed I'd put together out of six cinder blocks, two doors, and a mattress. Unlike Jeff's house, this one had three full bathrooms.

Living apart felt right to both Jeff and me. Seeing each other every Wednesday night and on weekends was enough. But we fought a lot. Not about housework or sexist language or other issues much discussed at the time, though. Jeff was no male chauvinist. He did the dishes and the laundry. He belonged to a men's group, five friends who met weekly to discuss the ideas of the women's movement and how men should change their lives. (They also went to ball games together). He respected women and never dismissed them. In fact, his ability to form warm attachments with women—and his eagerness to do so—sometimes made me uncomfortable. Still, it was hard for us to feel at ease with each other, and our time together was full of fireworks.

One evening, I showed up at his house after a long day and sank onto his mattress on the floor.

"You're in a foul mood," he observed.

"I just need some affection," I snapped.

He fell asleep.

Trying to wriggle away, was he? Just like Mr. K. from the Chamber of Commerce. I delivered a hard punch to his gut.

That woke him up. Not for the first time, he accused me of being a howitzer. (I had to look it up in the dictionary: a short-barreled cannon, used especially in World War I.) I didn't feel like a howitzer. I felt powerless. The whole business of being strong, but not too strong, and the varying messages coming in from Jeff and Karen and the Midwest Academy and society at large—all of this was a mystery to me. I was in over my head. Why couldn't I make things right? In my organizing work, the difference between "fair" and "unfair" seemed clear. But not here, not to me. Apparently, you couldn't browbeat someone into wanting to be with you.

I thought about the brochure we'd put out advising office workers on "how to get the respect you deserve." Start by asking for what you want, we counseled. Speak firmly and without hostility. Be matter-of-fact and positive. Give concrete reasons to back up your requests. Know your worth. Be confident. Take risks. Negotiate, barter, insist.

Was this how I should be behaving with my boyfriend? One evening when Jeff was supposed to come over but didn't, I waited a while, then called him.

"The house meeting is still going on," he said brusquely. All the group houses held monthly meetings, but while the meetings at my house focused on practical matters like dirty dishes in the kitchen sink, Jeff's house meetings were heavy on psychodrama and lasted for hours.

He sounded grumpy and cold, and I laid into him as usual. Later I wondered whether instead of pitching a fit I should have tried a different tack. What would happen if I tried following our organization's advice by speaking firmly and without hostility, being matter-of-fact and positive?

Him: The house meeting is still going on.

Me: Oh, I'm sorry. I'd like to talk. Can you spare a minute now, or what's a better time?

I wasn't sure this was the answer, and if it was, I wasn't sure if I could carry it off. But mindful of the parallels with my work at 9 to 5, I kept trying. We were encouraging women to find their voice and ask for what they wanted without blowing the whole place up—to improve their working conditions while keeping their jobs. We were encouraging them to take action as a group, but to each individual woman the situation no doubt felt deeply personal.

Three hundred women came to our hearing in April 1974. All the seats in the hall were filled, with overflow in the balcony. The government agencies all sent representatives who took seats on the stage, and the state legislature presented us with a citation congratulating us for our efforts. Seven women testified, each representing a different industry—insurance, banking, publishing, colleges and universities, temporary work, health care, and law firms. Getting up in front of a crowd was scary for all of them, and we held many practice sessions. For those who were afraid they might throw up at the podium, we suggested bringing along a small wastebasket, just in case.

No one did end up bringing a wastebasket, and in the end they all spoke up loud and clear. The reporter for the *Globe* characterized them as "articulate, coolly sarcastic, determined."

First came the statistical evidence—the hard proof of unfair and illegal conditions in Boston that Mr. K. at the Chamber of Commerce had asked us to send him. (Not that he or anyone else from the chamber was there to listen.) Women office workers were nearly one-quarter of the Boston-area workforce, and the figures told the story of our grievances:

- Women workers in the Boston area are as educated as men. Both sexes have more than twelve years of education on average. Yet female high school graduates working full-time make less than men who have not completed elementary school.
- Women of color make up only 4 percent of the clerical work-force.
- Only 22 percent of women working in Boston's offices hold professional, technical, managerial, or administrative jobs.
- Women are 74 percent of the clerical workforce, yet we earn only 64 percent of the pay.
- Boston has the highest cost of living in the country, yet we receive the lowest wages of women office workers in any northern city. Of the fifteen largest cities in the United States, only Memphis and Birmingham pay less.
- Office work in Boston pays less than factory work.

An insurance company employee reported that while her industry was pulling in profits in the double digits, the women at the firm saw their wages increase by only 2.2 percent a year. A legal secretary said that much of the work that clients paid for—research, tax filings, and so on—was done by secretaries. "The client pays $1,500 for the job. The secretary gets $16." "Female editorial assistants," said a speaker from the publishing industry, "train male editors who take home six-figure annual salaries."

Having presented the problems, we moved on to the solutions. Here in the city that called itself the "Cradle of Liberty," we'd invited our members to draft a Bill of Rights for Women Office Workers. (The original Bill of Rights, which became the first ten amendments to the US Constitution, was proposed by John Hancock in 1791 on the site now occupied by the First National Bank of Boston.) Our members had jumped at the idea. They got to ten items, couldn't stop, and ended up with thirteen. We had the document transcribed in elegant calligraphy and printed on sepia-colored stock that looked as venerable as parchment.

"We will rock the boat until the standards of the Bill of Rights for Women Office Workers are met," our final speaker proclaimed. Everyone at the hearing got a copy to take back to the office. Two state senators and a city councilor signed it, and another legislator promised to introduce it as a resolution on the floor of the State House. The next day it appeared in full in the *Boston Herald*.

HUNDREDS OF BOSTON'S SECRETARIES ARE ON THE WARPATH, read the headline in the *Christian Science Monitor*.

But were we? We still hadn't succeeded in "engaging the enemy." Employers were out there somewhere, but we hadn't been able to lure them into the open. Not a single one had attended our hearing. The Chamber of Commerce had asked us for proof of the problems but hadn't shown up to hear about them. Our members still hadn't had an opportunity to push for something and win.

It was time to "vie for power," but we couldn't figure out how.

The Bill of Rights for Women Office Workers

1. The right to respect as women and as office workers.
2. The right to comprehensive, written job descriptions specifying the nature of all duties expected of the employee.
3. The right to detailed descriptions specifying compensation, terms, conditions, and benefits of employment.
4. The right to compensation for overtime work and for work not included in our job descriptions.
5. The right to choose whether to do the personal work of employers (typing personal letters, serving coffee, running out for lunch).
6. The right to defined and regular salary reviews and cost-of-living raises.
7. The right to comprehensive medical coverage for any temporary medical disability without jeopardizing our seniority, benefits, or pensions.
8. The right to maternity benefits and to having pregnancy and other gynecological conditions treated as temporary medical disabilities.
9. The right to benefits equal to those of men in similar job categories.
10. The right to equal access to promotion opportunities and on-the-job training programs.
11. The freedom to choose one's lifestyle and to participate in on-the-job organizing or outside activities which do not detract from the execution of assigned tasks.
12. An end to discrimination on the basis of sex, age, race, marital status, or parenthood, as ensured by the laws of the Commonwealth of Massachusetts.
13. The right to written and systematic grievance procedures.

6

TEETERING FOR OUR RIGHTS

WOMEN WERE AFRAID OF LOSING THEIR JOBS. They were afraid of being ridiculed or yelled at by their bosses. But fear of the boss was not the only hard thing. Even some of our most enthusiastic members hesitated to talk to their coworkers about our organization. They were afraid of being shunned as fanatics, man-haters, crazies. We understood those fears, and we also knew that employers encouraged such views and benefited from them.

There were other obstacles as well. Many office workers were confined inside steel and concrete fortresses that were surrounded by privately owned sidewalks and sometimes patrolled by security guards. Inside, they weren't allowed to congregate. Supervisors could see everything that went on in the typing pools. The downtown streets emptied out at five and were dead after dark. Many women had to get home to their "second shift" of housework and childcare. Only those who had few such responsibilities became active in our organization. Others couldn't spare the time.

At first the women we were meeting were reluctant even to do things we considered relatively easy, like handing out the newsletter at T exits. They weren't up for the brusque turndowns, the risk of running into someone who might disapprove, the questions—"Whatcha sellin' today?"—that could feel harsh even if they weren't intended that way. Leaving a stack of leaflets in the ladies' room sounded low risk to us, but not everyone saw it that way. What if you got caught?

Maybe in neighborhood organizing you could look around for people who could take leadership and there they would be—people who held positions of responsibility in a church, a block association, a union, a local charity, or a political party. But within the office workforce there appeared to be no networks, no getting together, no history of speaking on behalf of others. Instead of finding whole offices full of discontented folks who wanted to get together to make change, we noticed that for the most part, women were coming to us one by one.

So the assumption that women in offices would be activated en masse had to go, along with many other notions. We were going to have to be less like a motorboat, setting a straight course, and more like a sailboat, sensing the wind. The leaders who emerged from our membership, it seemed, would be made, not found.

Little by little, we began to figure it out. We knew people's fears from the inside, and we drew on our own experience in encouraging them to step up. Remembering how I used to feel about making phone calls, I wrote scripts for women to use when they made turnout calls for our meetings. Janet, who'd played at piano recitals starting at the age of seven, remembered hoping she would fall down the steps and break her arm so she wouldn't have to go out onstage. She knew what it was to be shy, and that made her good at helping other shy people.

We broke everything down into discrete tasks—hand out the surveys, compile the figures, write the reports, prepare the statements—and doled out responsibilities in small bites: come to a meeting, bring a friend to the next meeting, welcome newcomers at the third, make a brief presentation at the fourth. A movement can feel like an army, with everyone going in one direction, but we made a point of paying attention to women as individuals, designing diverse roles for a range of personalities. Some women were out front, making speeches and leading demonstrations. Others were behind the scenes, gathering information, researching corporate structure. Some spoke up loudly. Others quietly set up chairs, welcomed others, made sure everyone was heard, encouraged the timid, thanked and praised. There were plenty of opportunities to move from one role to another.

As we staffers became adept at sensing what each individual was willing to do, what it would take to get her from point A to point B, more women began to be active and to blossom. They were eager to be recognized, to develop new skills, to feel respected, to make history, to take revenge.

By the beginning of the summer, we'd assembled a leadership core—Charlotte, Dottie, Carol, Kathy, Peg, and Fran—all of whom we'd met over lunch, and all of whom now felt committed to the organization. "A few months ago," they'd say as they took on one new task after another, "I would never have imagined myself doing this."

As time went by, our staff expanded too. Judith McCullough came to us from an insurance company, where a man in her department had been hired as a clerical worker, trained by a woman, and then quickly promoted over her, because, as the supervisor explained, "he has a family to support." Bathroom breaks were timed. Judy had once been sent home from work because the top of her pants suit didn't match the bottom. Two women had nearly been fired for discussing their salaries with others (a big no-no throughout the office workforce). There'd been talk of forming a union, but the women were scared and didn't know where to start. Judith hadn't seen a place for herself in the women's movement before, but she soon found herself becoming a respected spokeswoman on employment issues. After her experience on the 9 to 5 staff, she went on to a career in the labor movement.

Maureen O'Donnell, too, joined us full-time, fed up after her boss told her that she was the most important person in the office and that without her he'd have no idea what to do. It went without saying that neither her salary nor her title reflected that reality. At 9 to 5, though the pay still left something to be desired (the money we'd begun to receive from foundation grants and individual donors didn't allow for more than small staff salaries), she got the respect and recognition she'd never found in her office job.

Along with our growing staff and leadership group, we had press clippings we could use to raise money from funders and show to prospective members. The phone rang nonstop as women called for help with job problems. Newspapers and TV and radio stations wanted interviews. But after months of hard work, we still hadn't "engaged with the enemy," aside from our tepid meeting—OK, our outright defeat—at the hands of Mr. K. at the Chamber of Commerce.

It was time—past time. But we were still stumped.

And all the hard work had taken its toll. After nine months on the job, I found myself flagging. Too many meetings, too many words. I was tired of coddling and cajoling. On the T at the end of the day, I would try to calm myself with deep breathing, but even that felt like too much work. I needed a vacation.

Jeff and I began making plans for what seemed like an extreme get-away—a whole month just to ourselves. I felt guilty about needing a break, but Steve, from the Midwest Academy, gave me his blessing. Taking a vacation, he wrote, was a sign of maturity in an activist: "You no longer seem to feel you have to work harder than anyone else to save the world from itself." I was afraid Karen might disapprove, but she didn't. "Vacations are a good thing," she pronounced. "Go and enjoy yourself."

At the end of June, we drove up to a weather-beaten house on a mountainside in Nova Scotia. The weather was chilly, and the little house had neither heat nor running water, but it was heaven. The air smelled like roses and the fields were full of wild strawberries. The blue sky with its puffy clouds towered over the pines, and the sea glittered on the horizon. We slept late, went to the beach and immersed ourselves in the icy water, and lay in the sun. We learned the names of wildflowers—cow vetch, touch-me-not, eyebright, pearly everlasting. We learned the birds too—the barn swallow, the red-winged blackbird, and best of all, the white-throated sparrow with its poignant song: "Oh, sweet Canada, Canada, Canada." We played dominoes, Scrabble, cribbage. We read poetry and memoirs and novels about eras of tumultuous social change. We picked blueberries and baked pies. We took long walks during which we filled each other in on everything about our childhoods. Long, intimate talks were our "language of love," and we indulged in plenty of them. In the evenings, we watched the sky turn pink, then gray. We saw the green and red stripes of the northern lights and learned the constellations in the huge black sky: Cassiopeia, Cygnus the swan, the Big Dipper, Perseus, and Draco the dragon.

Our interpersonal battles didn't disappear. There was the usual see-saw of intimacy and warmth followed by distance and anger. But the abundance of time together felt like a feast. There were no telephones, no alarm clocks. The quiet seeped into our bones. An ease crept over us.

Day after day, I sat on the windy bluff overlooking the water and reflected on my life. Being an organizer, for me, meant working not only full-time but overtime and always staying on task. Now, though, I felt a hankering for the good things in life. I didn't want more money. I'd grown up in a family that worried about getting by but always managed, and I had no trouble living on my tiny salary. But something was missing. I found myself fantasizing about delicious meals served on special plates, arty clothes sewn from interesting fabrics, rooms painted in deep colors and filled with exotic objects—feathery plants in urns, beaded curtains—a life where everything I touched was stylish and full of beauty.

A quotation from one of my favorite authors came to mind. "I arise in the morning," wrote E. B. White, "torn between a desire to improve—or *save*—the world and a desire to enjoy—or *savor*—the world. This makes it hard to plan the day."

Upon moving to Boston after college, I'd stowed away in a virtual attic many of the things I'd once considered to be at the core of my being. I'd been brought up listening to classical music and reading the *New York Times Book Review* every Sunday. I'd learned to care deeply about painters like Matisse and Bonnard. Classic works of literature had been sacred to me. Now, as I sat in the sun, I missed the road not taken. The organizing life seemed to fit Karen like a glove, but for me it wasn't a perfect fit. "Save" or "savor"—which did I want? Did I have to choose?

Up there on my bluff, I also pondered what I referred to as the question of the duck and the wave. All this past year I'd been trying as hard as I could to master the techniques of organizing. But maybe the techniques didn't matter. Maybe *I* didn't matter. So much was out of my control. Maybe I was nothing but a duck riding on the surface of the water. Maybe all that mattered were the larger dynamics—the great waves of economic and cultural change that were crashing over today's workplace. The flight of capital out of heavy industry. The rise of office work. The movement of millions of women into the workforce. The influence of the civil rights movement in spurring unionizing in new sectors of the economy. Compared to these macro forces, maybe everything my friends and I were trying to do was trivial. How much impact did activists like me actually have? Maybe all our hard work would make a measurable difference, but maybe not.

Maybe Robert F. Kennedy had it right when he said this to young people in South Africa in 1966:

> Few will have the greatness to bend history itself; but each of us can work to change a small portion of events, and in the totality of all those acts will be written the history of this generation.
>
> Each time a man stands up for an ideal, or acts to improve the lot of others, or strikes out against injustice, he sends forth a tiny ripple of hope, and crossing each other from a million different centers of energy and daring, those ripples build a current that can sweep down the mightiest walls of oppression and resistance.

Maybe the answer was the duck *and* the wave. And maybe, too, I could save the world *and* savor the world.

"Can't wait for you to get back," Karen wrote. "Wait till you see what an impressive crew we make with your return." Her words made me feel good. When the month came to an end, we stowed a bucket of berries under the front seat and drove back to Boston. The vacation had been just what I needed, and now I found myself eager to get back into the fray.

———————

Things had changed at 9 to 5 while I was away. At last the organization had succeeded in jumping into the arena; the enemy had been engaged. The vehicle was a maternity benefits bill that was pending before the Massachusetts State Senate, which would require employers to treat pregnancy and childbirth like any other temporary disability—one of the planks in our Bill of Rights. As things stood, an employee at a typical company who broke a leg or needed a hernia operation was entitled to sick days and disability benefits. But an employee who had to miss work as a result of pregnancy or childbirth was a different story. Not all sick leave policies covered absences related to maternity. Not all health insurance plans covered pregnancy. You might have expected that this would be illegal, but it wasn't. Yes, the Civil Rights Act of 1964 outlawed race and sex discrimination in the workplace and required equal benefits for men and women, but somehow pregnancy was an exception. The new bill sought to eliminate this inequality, at least in Massachusetts.

Employers were up in arms. The biggest lobbyist against the bill, we discovered, was New England Telephone and Telegraph. Fortunately for us, the phone company had two vulnerabilities. Its employees were union members who had an extra layer of protection and were used to taking a stand. And because the company was a public utility, it was subject to a high degree of government oversight. These vulnerabilities were our strengths. We set about exploiting them.

The management of a semipublic entity *had* to respond to members of the public, so we sent a group of 9 to 5'ers on their lunch hour to meet with a room full of telephone executives. Acting as customers, not as employees, made it easier for our members to speak up. We presented two demands:

- Stop using customers' money to lobby against women's rights. Take the money out of company profits, or out of President William Mercer's $170,000 annual salary.
- Change the maternity benefits policy for phone company employees—now.

Next, we made common cause with the telephone employees' union and leafleted outside the doors of the company's main building. The 9 to 5 members who were leafleting didn't work for the phone company, so they didn't have to worry about running into their own bosses. And the phone company workers felt protected by their union contract. NEW ENGLAND TELEPHONE AND TELEGRAPH LOBBIES AGAINST WOMEN'S JOB RIGHTS, read our headline, atop a cartoon of a grouchy-looking boss sitting at a massive desk, with a thought balloon reading "Crab, crab, crab! What do those dumb broads want now?" The text, addressed to phone company workers in the name of both 9 to 5 and the union, read:

> New England Telephone, your employer, has spent thousands of dollars this year to lobby against maternity benefits bills at the State House. . . . If you are pregnant and will not receive disability pay, contact your union.

When we learned that the phone company had petitioned the Department of Public Utilities for a rate increase, we figured out a way to catch the decision makers by surprise. The DPU had never before considered the issue of discrimination in deciding about a rate increase, but there was always a first time. A posse of 9 to 5'ers went to the DPU on their lunch hour and demanded that no increase be granted "until NETT stops discriminating against women." Going after the regulator rather than the company helped our members overcome their fears. Again, it was much easier for them to holler at the DPU than at their boss, and they felt far safer protesting as ratepayers than as employees.

The DPU deliberated and sided with us, ruling that the company's lobbying costs could *not* be passed along in customers' phone bills. Instead, the company would have to dip into its profits. Victory!

In the end, Senate Bill 806 died in committee, and the phone company got its rate increase. Not until 1978 did the federal Pregnancy Discrimination Act give pregnant women throughout the country the same legal rights as other employees. With the passage of that law, employers could no longer refuse to hire or promote a pregnant woman who was capable of performing her job, nor could they demote or fire a woman for being pregnant. And a woman whose pregnancy made her unable to work was entitled to disability benefits or sick leave like any other employee.

Even though we ended up losing the maternity benefits fight that summer, our organization had turned a corner. We'd paid attention to women's reluctance to take action at their own workplaces, and we'd found ways around that constraint. Our members came to feel a new sense of identification with the organization and a new level of comfort with our activities. Members began bringing friends and coworkers with them to meetings. Our spokeswomen became more confident and effective than ever before.

That summer, women office workers became a new factor in Boston's political scene. We moved squarely into the public sphere and began to make our voices heard. In the months and years ahead, we spoke up and pressed for change, making use of multiple tactics and myriad pressure points to confront government and corporate power alike. Again and again, we surprised ourselves with our own eloquence, our own toughness, our own determination.

Maybe the turning point came during our first demonstration for the maternity bill at the State House. In front of the steps outside the venerable brick building with its gleaming gold dome, our members formed an uneven circle and began to move. Around and around they went, looking more nervous than militant. Then, suddenly, Fran Cicchetti broke into a chant: "Pass that bill! Pass that bill!" After a moment of uncertainty, faces lit up and everyone joined in. "Pass that bill! Pass that bill!" Voices rang out louder and louder, the circle picked up speed, and the TV cameras rolled.

Women in platform shoes carrying homemade picket signs—who would have imagined such a thing? We called it "teetering for our rights."

7

WHILE HE WAS
WEARING THEM

IN 1952 THE US DEPARTMENT OF COMMERCE designated the last full week in April as National Secretaries Week. Wednesday, the middle of the week, was National Secretaries Day—a time for bosses to present their secretaries with a dozen roses or a box of chocolates in gratitude for a year of hard work.

Really? A bouquet? A box of candy? We wanted our rights—our Bill of Rights—365 days a year. Echoing the call for "Bread and Roses" in the garment workers' song at the turn of the century, our slogan was Raises, Not Roses!—or sometimes Raises *and* Roses!

We set about taking over this "holiday" by inviting women to nominate their bosses in a citywide "Petty Office Procedures" contest. A petty office procedure was defined as anything that drove women workers up the wall—an unreasonable demand, a ridiculous rule, a non-job-related task, or an outrageous errand.

Nominations poured in. The winner was a boss who ordered his secretary to sew up a rip in his pants—while he was wearing them. We took a group of women on their lunch hour to present the man with an "executive sewing kit." TV cameras rolled as he sheepishly accepted the gift.

Soon after that, we heard from a secretary who'd been fired for bringing her boss, a lawyer, a corned beef sandwich on white bread instead of

Our slogan was Raises, Not Roses! *Karen Nussbaum*

rye. He refused to meet with us, but cameras rolled again as we picketed his office. Employers and employees across town heard all about the incident, and when the boss wouldn't back down, we filed a complaint with the Massachusetts Board of Bar Overseers. In vain. The woman didn't get her job back. When it came to a corned beef sandwich, apparently some infractions were unforgivable.

One day, Janet was on her way back to the office after a recruitment lunch when she ran into a woman dressed as a bumblebee who was handing out flyers for a small clothing store. It turned out that she'd been hired to work as a clerk in the store's back office, but a part of the job that wasn't mentioned in the interview was parading around the streets in this silly costume. The next day at noon we showed up at the store with a jar of honey for the manager. DON'T GET STUNG BY A PETTY BOSS! read our press release. The *Globe* published a front-page article about our visit to the store.

If there was something belittling about National Secretaries Day, well, we belittled right back. Some of the men we visited with our small mob of women and reporters wouldn't open the door. Others good-naturedly played along. The contests offered a quick and efficient education for both sides. Office workers who were afraid (so far) to confront the CEOs of the most powerful financial institutions in town found it possible— even fun—to spend their lunch hour twitting a hapless small business- man. Our tone at these press actions was light, gleeful, and indignant. By mocking the offending bosses as clueless buffoons, we brought them down a peg. A cartoon we printed in our newsletter depicted a boss seated in a baby's high chair banging his spoon. "Bring me my coffee!" he bawled. "Take my daughter shopping! Pick up my suit from the clean- ers! I'm a busy man!"

The reporters, some of whom were women experiencing similar prob- lems in their own work lives, got it. "Get my coffee, dear," an article in the *Globe* began. "Ring my wife for me, dear. Run out and pick up my cleaning, dear. Smile." One reporter went so far as to embed herself by signing up with a temp agency and going undercover in an office to find out what it was all about. Her eyes were opened. "My job behind the reception desk was to please and serve," she wrote. "When the executives came by, I'd say good morning. For the most part they ignored me or treated me like a child."

Many a boss seemed to assume that his secretary would do anything he asked. After all, he was the boss, wasn't he? We pushed back. Just as the manager was hired to perform tasks for the company, we argued, so was the secretary. Office workers were hired to type, file, schedule meet- ings, and take messages, not to cater to personal whims. We crafted a model personal errands policy, urging bosses to list all required duties in a written job description. And "if you must ask your secretary to perform duties that are not strictly job related," we said, "give her the opportunity to say no."

To secretaries, we said: "Learn to say no."

Some secretaries didn't mind doing personal errands. Getting up from the desk to fetch lunch for the boss could be a refreshing break. One woman wrote to us that her boss (a bachelor, she specified for some rea- son) had let her know from the start that "he needed and would pay for jobs outside the realm of an ordinary secretary's duties." She took the job under those conditions and had never regretted it, she said.

Others felt differently. A secretary whose job involved a lot of noncompany business—balancing her boss's checkbook, typing school assignments for his daughter, babysitting—wrote to say that at first, "my attitude was, it's his money, and if that's what he wanted me to do with my time, that was his business. Then I began to think about it. I am a professional. This is not professional work. It's keeping me from the already full-time duties I have in the office, and I have to work frantically to get them done."

Over the years, as we ran our "bad boss" contests all over the country, nominations involving pants were a constant. There was the boss who beckoned his secretary into the men's room to pin up the broken zipper on his fly, and there was the one who took *off* his pants and stood by while his secretary sewed on a button. There was the one who asked his secretary to write to the manufacturer of his underpants to complain that they bunched up in the crotch—and mail back the used underwear. The one who required his secretary to do his laundry, including boxers and jockstrap. And the one who asked his secretary to return a pair of his wife's pantyhose to a store.

More on trousers: Boston's mayor, Kevin White, won favor in our eyes when he proclaimed April 25 as "9 to 5 Day" in our honor. Not long afterward, though, he issued a directive ordering the city's female employees to wear skirts instead of pants. We were getting ready to honor him with the Boss of Yesteryear Award when he rescinded the order.

Many entries involved bodily fluids, private parts, or personal hygiene. The boss who asked his secretary to clean a spot off his tie was trumped by the one who handed his secretary a warm container of his own urine to carry to a lab, and that one was eclipsed by the one who asked his secretary to carry his *stool* sample to a doctor's office.

A boss asked his secretary to clean his dentures, another to vacuum up the fingernail clippings he'd scattered on the floor. One boss asked his secretary to wax his back hair, another to snip his nose hairs.

Sometimes the arrogance was breathtaking. A boss—I can't believe I'm writing this—required the secretaries in the office to cup their hands when he came into the room so that he could use them as ashtrays.

A boss sent his secretary outside to bargain with the meter maid, explaining why his car should not be ticketed. Another ordered his secretary to place illegal bets—without sharing in the winnings.

A boss returned from a fishing trip and announced that a bag full of fresh trout had leaked all over the upholstery of the company car. Her job: get rid of the smell.

A boss referred to his secretary as his "squaw." "My squaw will get back to you."

Women's intelligence was routinely overlooked. A boss asked his secretary what she was doing as she sat at her typewriter. "Thinking," she said. "Get back to work," he barked. "You're not paid to think."

A typing drill from the 1970s—a text for students to practice on while learning to type—went like this: "A secretary is nice to look at. She makes an office a pleasant place with her charm and her knack for adapting to the moods of others." An ad for a temporary employment agency showed a woman emerging from a wooden packing crate over the headline THE LAST WORD IN 1970 OFFICE EQUIPMENT. An ad for typewriters titled TRUE CONFESSIONS OF AN OLIVETTI GIRL featured a woman with a low-cut neckline and a come-hither expression. "Now that I type sharper," she was saying, "I *look* sharper." Worst yet, Karen remembered a magazine ad for a piece of office equipment that boasted, THIS MACHINE IS JUST LIKE YOUR SECRETARY: SILENT, EFFICIENT, AND EASILY MANIPULABLE.

"Bosses don't have day-to-day contact with the work," a secretary wrote us. "The clerical workers know better, but we aren't allowed to exercise our intelligence because it is assumed we have none."

A case in point: when a law office in Chicago redecorated, the attorneys had the secretaries' chairs bolted to the floor so they wouldn't mar the new carpet. Come Monday morning, the secretaries sat down at their desks and found they couldn't reach their typewriters or their phones.

Many bosses felt free to pass along their family responsibilities to their secretaries. A boss asked his secretary to explain to his mother why he could no longer come to dinner every Monday night. Another asked his secretary to pack his suitcases for a vacation. A third called his secretary at home during a snowstorm and told her to come to the office to babysit his kids, even though it meant leaving her own children home alone.

It wasn't just men. Women managers were at fault too. One secretary wrote that her female boss "flew by my desk in a flurry between meetings, threw a dollar on my desk and asked me to buy an anniversary card for her husband."

Some bosses put their secretaries at the disposal of their family members. A boss asked his secretary to accompany his wife, an interior designer, to a job site and measure a room for an expensive rug. Another promised his daughter that if she did well on her report card, she'd be allowed to dictate a book report to his secretary. A third asked his secretary not only to type his daughter's term paper but to write it.

Dogs played a starring role in the contests. A boss asked his secretary to drive his sick dog to the vet. Another ordered his secretary to write an anonymous letter to a neighbor to complain about a barking dog. But first (did this make any sense?) she had to drive across the state line to make sure the letter had a mystery postmark.

While bosses routinely imported their family responsibilities into the office, secretaries' family responsibilities were strictly unwelcome. "I asked to use my vacation time when my son was in the hospital with appendicitis," a woman wrote. "My boss flew into a rage and said, 'If your family is more important to you than your job, you're not the right person for this company.'"

Coffee was a major, major issue. One of our early posters showed a coffee cup on its side with a little puddle dribbling out. No explanation needed.

In 1977 a Chicago legal secretary named Iris Rivera was fired for refusing to make the coffee. When protesters from Women Employed, the working women's group, visited her boss and demanded her reinstatement, the incident made headlines not only citywide, and not only nationwide, but around the world. She got her job back.

In 1979 at the *Cleveland Press*, female copy aides—*only* females—were required to fetch coffee for the male editors. Members of our thriving chapter in Cleveland paid a noontime visit to the paper, bringing with them an eight-foot-long scroll telling editors how to make their own

coffee. The paper covered the event with the headline THANKS, BUT YOU
SHOULDN'T HAVE. The policy was discontinued.

In Seattle in 1978, an office worker named Cassandra E. Amesley
wrote these lyrics to the tune of the traditional American song "Simple
Gifts."

> If you're too important to make coffee or tea
> Well, that sure says what you think of me
> If the logic in this song doesn't filter through
> You drip, I still have grounds to sue

For the most part, the newspapers tended to cover us on the business
page, which few office workers read. This forced us to dream up ever
more creative antics to try to make it into the news or features section.
Boston's City Hall Plaza, where we held our National Secretaries Week
festivities, was an organizer's nightmare—a huge, windswept expanse with
city hall squatting at one end and the Federal Building reaching for the
sky at the other. The place sucked up audio and made any crowd smaller
than a thousand look tiny. One year we positioned dozens of members
throughout the plaza and had them pass out tens of thousands of green
"Working Women's Dollars" marked "59 cents"—the gap between men's
and women's wages at the time. Another year we built a giant coffee
cup and parked it in the middle of the plaza. A third year it was a giant
typewriter. One year we had our members release four hundred helium
balloons into the sky, each bearing the slogan UP WITH 9 TO 5! RIGHTS
AND RESPECT! I still remember the wonderful squeaking and whispering
of the balloons overhead before they left our hands—and then the logisti-
cal difficulty of trying to get into a taxi with the half dozen balloons we'd
saved to decorate our office at the Y. (Back then, we were unaware of the
dangers that balloons pose to wildlife.)

In 1975 a women's rock band called the Deadly Nightshade got in
touch and offered to hold a noonday concert on our behalf on National
Secretaries Day. They erected a stage and set up a pair of enormous amps.
The sound attracted a huge crowd, and the songs were right on the nose.
In one, a secretary interviews her former boss, Mr. Big, who has ended
up on the unemployment line:

Well, hello, Mr. Big, remember me?
. . . .
Well, can you type? Oh no?
Can you file? Oh no?
And no, you cannot take dictation?

A wooden puppet then tap-danced across the stage as the singer brayed, "Dance, Mr. Big, dance!" The crowd roared.

Our most ambitious National Secretaries Week endeavor, in 1976, was a "tag week," which involved hiring dozens of people to fan out across the city and ask passersby for donations on behalf of working women's rights. Anyone who put a dollar in the can got a button with a white rose on a red background. Monday, when the brigade of taggers started their week, was balmy and fragrant, one of the first warm days of spring. The tag team members smiled and basked in the sunshine, and the cash poured in. But by Tuesday, typically for April in New England, the weather had turned gusty, chilly, and gray. The taggers shivered and hopped from foot to foot. Even so, by the end of the week they'd brought in thousands of dollars.

The tag week was so successful that we repeated it for several years running. Building on that success, we launched a summerlong door-to-door canvassing program. Everyone on the 9 to 5 staff was required to take a shift for a few nights along with the hired canvassers. Remembering the disastrous evening I'd spent knocking on doors for a community group when I was a student at the Midwest Academy, I expected the worst when my turn came. To my surprise, this time around I loved it. By now I was a different person. I believed deeply in the organization I was representing, and my enthusiasm came through when I asked people to support the cause.

While our shenanigans during the last full week of April were great fun, a serious thread ran through them. And over the years, the kinds of entries we received in our bad boss contests began to shift from the laughable to the painful.

We heard about firings—abusive ones. A secretary came back from vacation and lost her job for having put on a few pounds. Another logged in to her computer and learned of her termination on the screen. There was the boss who phoned his secretary in the hospital to tell her she'd been let go. And the boss who returned from vacation and ordered all his staff members to enroll in the program of intensive "personal growth" of which he'd become a devotee. Those who refused were forced to resign. "My only regret," wrote the secretary who told us about this one, "was the loss of my non-vested pension."

Some contest entries involved serious illness, danger, even death. From MIT, the male bastion across the river in Cambridge, came this story: "A woman from down the hall burst into the office. She said she was feeling sick and fell to the floor. Just then a professor who was a world-renowned authority in his field opened the door. He looked down at the woman, stepped over her body to get to the file cabinet, stepped back over her body, and left the room."

A boss and his secretary were toiling at their desks when a suspicious-looking envelope arrived in the mail. "This could be a letter bomb," the boss said. "*You* open it."

A fire broke out in an office. The woman at the help desk was ordered to stay at her post and keep answering the phones while smoke filled the room.

A woman was just starting her shift when she received a phone call saying her mother had died. She tried to keep working, but her emotions caught up with her. She told her boss what had happened. "Well," he said, "there's nothing you can do now. You may as well stay."

A woman received a phone call from her hysterical children and raced home to find the babysitter dead on the sofa. Her boss, a doctor, demanded that she return to the office. She didn't go back. Ever.

The ultimate "personal errand," of course, was a demand for sexual favors. The term *sexual harassment* was coined in 1975, but even before the term became widely used, the problem was evident everywhere. My story about the professor who wanted me to type up the history of all his blow jobs was matched and surpassed by many others.

We heard from a secretary whose boss invited her to lunch, and then, on the way to the restaurant, told her to walk over a steam vent so that he could see what color underwear she was wearing.

A boss brought his son to the office and ordered his secretary to take him out on a date. She protested that she was engaged to be married (not that she should have needed such a reason—or any reason—for saying no), but the boss was unmoved.

A boss routinely tucked his secretary's paycheck into the waistline of his pants and made her pluck it out.

A boss left for a trip overseas and asked his secretary to send love notes to his girlfriend while he was away.

A boss equipped his secretary with a beeper and sent her to a nearby bar, with instructions to let him know if any "hot babes" showed up.

A receptionist wrote in that she had to work at a desk surrounded by pornographic posters.

An office party featured a cake baked in the form of two breasts. The boss wielded the knife and passed out the slices.

Worse, a woman was raped by her boss. Another was raped by a coworker—then fired.

In 1977 for the first time a federal court upheld a charge of sexual harassment, in a case in which a government employee was dismissed and her job was abolished when she refused to perform sexual favors for her boss. In 1980 the Equal Employment Opportunity Commission (EEOC) issued guidelines establishing that sexual harassment was a form of sex discrimination. And in the fall of 1991, the issue became a matter of national news during US Senate hearings on the nomination of Clarence Thomas for the Supreme Court. A former employee, Anita Hill, testified that while she worked as his assistant, he had subjected her to years of unwelcome sexual attention. The hearings were carried live on TV, and viewers were riveted, just as they would be in 2019 when Supreme Court nominee Brett Kavanaugh was accused of sexual assault during his Senate hearings.

During the hearings, sexual harassment began to be discussed everywhere. What is it? How do you pronounce it? Why does it happen? Whose responsibility is it to stop it? That week we received six thousand calls on our toll-free job hotline. Perhaps the most poignant came from a woman whose voice trembled as she disclosed that her boss had harassed her and that she had never told anyone about it until now. When had this happened? "1954," she whispered.

Surveys confirmed that millions of women were receiving unwanted sexual attention on the job. Within a year of the hearings, the number of

sexual harassment complaints filed with the EEOC had risen by 50 percent. An increasing number of Americans believed Hill's word over Thomas's, and an increasing number of companies began implementing policies
to curb sexual harassment.

Soon after the hearings, Ellen Bravo, who directed our chapter in
Milwaukee, and I wrote *The 9 to 5 Guide to Combating Sexual Harassment*, which offered advice to employees and employers alike. We
defined what sexual harassment is: repeated, unwanted, intimidating,
uncomfortable sexual attention at the workplace. Such behavior, we
stressed, is illegal. We also discussed what sexual harassment is *not*:
mutually enjoyable banter, flirting, or romance. (Some workplaces set
ground rules regarding dating between coworkers, or between managers
and subordinates.) And we laid out the most effective factors that help
to stop sexual harassment:

1. Written policies that provide multiple channels for reporting and
    redress, a range of discipline, and protection of both accusers
    and accused.
2. Men learning to pay attention, listen, and ask themselves how a
    wife, daughter, or sister would feel if subjected to sexual atten-
    tion on the job.
3. Women learning to trust their instincts and say no, seek and
    give support, use company channels, file complaints, speak out
    and speak up.

Sexual harassment doesn't occur in a vacuum, we emphasized. It's part
and parcel of women's lack of power on the job. The more the subject is
out in the open and addressed in the context of women's job rights as a
whole, the better.

Anita Hill's testimony broke a long-standing silence. Her testimony
ignited a national discussion. Decades later, the discussion is still going
on. Countless lawsuits have been filed. Countless high-profile bosses have
been dismissed for inappropriate behavior. As the #MeToo movement
makes clear, sexual harassment is still widespread in the workplace. And
employees still need to join together to stop it.

Back in the 1970s, the idea that a man could order his "girl" to satisfy his every fancy began to go the way of the manual typewriter. The old office culture began to crumble. "The image of the loyal, quiet, grateful secretary living in her boss's shadow at one fourth the pay," said an article in the *Globe* in 1974, "is cracking fast."

And we were about to hit our stride.

8

IN OUR GLORY! (PART I): "WE THINK A LOT OF WOMEN . . ."

At our hearing in the spring of 1974, women had spoken up about the problems in Boston's key office industries. But simply naming the problems was not enough. We wanted to solve them. Could women in these industries join together to make change? It was time to find out.

We divided up the job. Janet and Judith would work with women in insurance and banking, Karen would work with women in colleges and universities, and I'd work with women in the publishing industry.

Publishing was a natural fit for me. To the extent that I'd ever been able to see myself making a living as an adult, I'd pictured something involving the printed word. But now, instead of sitting behind an editorial desk, I hunkered down in my cubicle at the Y and set to work trying to figure out how to make the publishing industry change its ways. A handy reference book called *Literary Market Place*, which I found at the public library, listed all the publishers in town—textbook publishers, general-audience "trade" publishers, and magazine publishers of all kinds—along with the names and phone numbers of employees up and down the hierarchy. In no time at all, we had a robust network of contacts across the industry.

Publishing in Boston was second only to New York in size and importance, and it carried a certain prestige. About 3,500 people, most of them women, worked in the several dozen companies that produced books and periodicals in the Boston area. Everybody knew everybody, and information flew swiftly from firm to firm. The women I met loved books, expected to spend their lives in the industry, and were proud of the works they helped to shepherd from proposal to finished product.

But the more phone calls I made, the more leads I followed up on, the more lunches I ate—the more distressed I became over the picture that emerged. To a large extent, women's dreams were thwarted. Many had degrees in literature, and even if they started at the bottom of the career ladder, they expected to move up. Yet men seemed to have a lock on the top positions. As one woman testified at our April hearing, even if you had an impressive title like "assistant editor," you were likely to remain near the bottom of the career ladder, training men who would soon be making more money than you ever would. In many ways, conditions were ideal for organizing. Almost all the publishing houses were located downtown, including two big ones right across from the Boston Common, and this made it easy for women to get to meetings. Unlike in the big finance companies, employees could leave their desks without being penalized. And women were itching to make change, eager to make use of skills—strategizing, researching, writing, deciding—that weren't being tapped on the job.

As everyone in the Boston publishing industry was aware, several union drives were in progress at publishing companies in New York City. There was even a strike brewing down there. But Boston was different. The women who showed up at our first get-togethers were enthusiastic about taking some kind of action, but they were far from militant—at least at first.

We kicked around some ideas. The *Boston Globe* Book Festival was coming up—an annual event that drew everyone in the industry and thousands of members of the public. It was a perfect venue for getting the word out about grievances among publishing employees. I suggested throwing up a picket line outside the festival entrance. A long moment of silence greeted that idea before someone politely raised the alternative notion of renting a table inside the festival and handing out a survey.

We did rent a table, and dozens of women clamored for the chance to take a turn staffing it. The job survey we designed was passed around at every publishing company in town, and we had no trouble assembling a team to analyze it and write up the results.

Around this time, I received a letter from my mother praising the progress we were making. "9 to 5," she said, "sounds more influential, bolder, brassier, stronger, bigger, and more active every time you write." But a bold, brassy organization was the last thing these women wanted to be associated with. 9 to 5 was too radical for them, they told me. They wanted their own group with its own name: "Women in Publishing," or WIP, pronounced like "whip."

They didn't like the word *meeting*, which sounded too aggressive, and instead insisted on the word *gathering*. They wouldn't hold their gatherings at the Y, where 9 to 5 met, preferring a church basement around the corner from the two flagship publishing houses. There, the gatherings were packed.

Rather than posting their news in the 9 to 5 bimonthly newsletter, they produced a two-sided sheet of their own, full of carefully worded commentary on the industry, and circulated it across town. I thought the sheet was dry and boring, but it got a tremendous response. After the first issue came out, we received an unsolicited check in the mail for fifty dollars. Unheard of!

I was worried sick. The whole effort had taken off much faster than I'd expected, and I didn't have a firm hand on the reins. But fortunately, despite my missteps (the suggestion about the picket line being a prime example), the women wanted me involved. I made clear that if I were to be part of WIP, then WIP would have to be part of 9 to 5. They agreed that every flyer, every report, every press release would bear both names: "Women in Publishing/9 to 5."

As we got closer to our first public event, where we would release the results of our survey, I learned that Julie, the chair of WIP, had been scheduling lunchtime get-togethers without my knowledge, with the goal of making sure that the tone of the upcoming evening would be very different from the "abrasive" tone of 9 to 5 as a whole. "We want to work *with* the companies, not against them," she was telling everyone. Another key member of the group suddenly resigned, saying that the event was shaping up to be far too confrontational for her tastes. I tried to coax her back in, but she held firm. Yes, she agreed, all the women at her company were clustered at the bottom, but the company wasn't actually breaking any *laws*, was it? And even if it were, in her view filing discrimination charges would be jumping the gun.

I started having dreams about WIP every night. Nightmares. Was the whole effort too mild? Was I being too soft? What would Heather and Steve say? Many WIP members were higher on the class ladder than 9 to 5 members in other industries. Was that OK? I almost lost it one evening when an ultrarefined looking WIP member sailed into one of our gatherings wearing a fur coat and carrying an armload of daffodils. I couldn't bring myself to report this disturbing moment to Karen and Janet, though I did describe it to Jeff when I got home. "What have I gotten myself into?" I wailed.

On the evening of that first public event, in March 1975, I stood in the doorway of the church basement and watched as three hundred people crowded into the room. Most were women, but unlike at our earlier city-wide hearing, this time men from top management made it their business to attend. As one woman after another strode to the podium to present our findings and our goals, the men listened intently.

"Behind the publishing industry's glamorous image," our report stated, "lurks a grim reality of unfair and illegal policies." Among our discoveries were these:

- Women in publishing are channeled into secretarial jobs and editorial jobs, while men are channeled into sales jobs—a prerequisite for getting into management—with higher salaries and commissions.
- Women are 66 percent of the employees in the industry but hold only 6 percent of management jobs.
- Male college graduates entering publishing start out with salaries of $3,000+ more than women college graduates.
- As the years pass, men's salaries keep climbing relative to those of women with comparable experience.
- Being a man in publishing is worth an extra $3,500 a year.

"WIP hopes," the report concluded, "that this report will open communication channels between management and women employees . . . so that the two groups can act together to bring about meaningful change. Only then can the myth of a glamorous career in publishing be exchanged for a challenging and fulfilling reality."

I personally wasn't sure about these sentiments. "The two groups can act together"? Wasn't that a bit starry-eyed? Wasn't it much too optimistic to think that the powers that be would want to "act together" with their employees to "bring about meaningful change"? I recalled the words of the great abolitionist Frederick Douglass that I'd learned at the Midwest Academy:

> If there is no struggle there is no progress. Those who profess to favor freedom and yet deprecate agitation are men who want crops without plowing up the ground; they want rain without thunder and lightning. They want the ocean without the awful roar of its many waters. . . . Power concedes nothing without a demand. It never did and it never will.

Weren't the women of WIP doomed to defeat if they persisted in trying to make common cause with their employers? Didn't they need to get out there and voice their demands with thunder and lightning and an awful roar?

It soon became clear that my fears were misplaced. Daffodils and all, these women knew what they were doing. They were smart, strategic, and brave. They knew when the light touch was the right touch, and they also knew when to get tough. They had their own ideas about *how* they wanted to struggle, but they were more than ready to get into the ring. Immediately after we released our report, a group of WIP members sat down to evaluate all the "handles" we could use to press for change. There were many.

Boston was not only the capital of Massachusetts but also the biggest city in New England. As such, it was the regional seat of the federal government. So we had easy access to all the city, state, and federal offices we could possibly want. We had two liberal US senators, a liberal mayor, and a newly elected Democratic governor. Boston politics back then was a lively mix of blue-blooded elites, Irish and Italian pols, and a tiny cadre of Black elected officials who could always be counted on to support our efforts. (Over the years, Boston's demographics changed, with rising numbers of Black, Latino, and Asian residents, and politicians reflecting that diversity.)

Out of all the available characters, we zeroed in on one. The new attorney general, Frank Bellotti, was a scrappy politician who spoke often about having felt the sting of anti-Italian bias as a child. Upon taking office, he'd announced himself as the head of the "people's law firm." He moved his office out of the State House, away from the lobbyists and the lawmakers, and started hiring women. During his twelve-year tenure, the number of women in the AG's office rose from four to eighty-four.

We set up a meeting with one of these women appointees and presented her with a copy of our report on the publishing industry. Within a week, we heard back that Bellotti was prepared to join us in filing a class action suit against one or more companies. A class action suit was a way to seek redress for a large group of employees who'd suffered from sex and/or race discrimination. To move forward, we'd need plaintiffs—individuals who had experienced discrimination personally and who were willing to be publicly named. But the suits would not benefit these individuals alone. The named plaintiffs would serve as representatives of the whole "class" of aggrieved employees. The point was to change job conditions for all.

The women of WIP leafleted up a storm and waited to see if anyone would come forward.

While waiting, we got busy—and sassy. We presented Dubious Distinction Awards, including a "Wasted Woman Power Award," to several publishers, spotlighting the worst maternity leave policies, the worst salary review policies, the worst promotion policies. We leafleted the shareholders' meeting of one big publisher. We sent letters to sixteen school boards around the country, urging them not to buy books from companies that discriminated.

WIP members and 9 to 5 members from other industries also devoted time to learning how federal affirmative action regulations could work for us. An agency called the Office of Federal Contract Compliance (later, for some reason, changed to the Office of Federal Contract Compliance *Programs*, or OFCCP), was in charge of administering Executive Order 11246, issued by President Lyndon B. Johnson in 1965. The order aimed to remedy discrimination on the basis of sex, race, religion, and national origin by requiring government contractors to take positive steps—"affirmative action"—to correct the effects of past discriminatory practices. Companies with fifty employees or more that did at least $50,000 of business with the federal government had to write affirmative action plans, or AAPs, in which they described the composition of their workforce (how many people of what sex and race worked in what positions), pinpointed problem areas, and laid out specific goals and timetables for improvement. The idea was to achieve measurable results by hiring and promoting women and people of color into positions from which they had been excluded.

The program offered a golden opportunity for opening up jobs and career ladders to groups that had long been held back. And many of the remedies recommended by the government—clear job descriptions and job requirements, job posting, job training, and clear promotion avenues—were elements of good management that benefited all workers. Companies were required to share their affirmative action plans not only with employees but also with the general public, and this meant we could look at management's own stated goals and use them to press for action. Unlike a lawsuit or a charge filed with the EEOC, this approach did not require individuals to come forward publicly. We could examine the AAP, demand that the company work toward its goals, and urge the government to make sure it happened.

The more research we did, however, the clearer it became that while the affirmative action program looked great on paper, in real life it fell short of its promise. We calculated that there were more than eight hundred Boston-area companies that had federal contracts exceeding $50,000, all required by law to file an affirmative action plan. Yet 40 percent of OFCCP's enforcement resources were allocated to the construction industry, which accounted for only 10 percent of the workforce in the Boston area. Enforcers were paying little attention to the office industries that dominated the Boston skyline, where women's advancement was blocked and people of color were nearly absent.

And although the regulations required employers to share their AAPs with employees, few women had ever heard of them. On the rare occasions when government investigators showed up to examine job conditions at a given company, they tended to talk only with management, not with employees. Reviews were cursory; enforcement was lax. Just how lax was driven home to us when we met with a roomful of affirmative action staffers at the Federal Building. One official fell asleep during the meeting, and those who remained awake told us that although enforcement was their job, they didn't actually believe in it. The real way to get employers to comply with the law, they explained, was not to make them do it but to try to convince them to do the right thing. Enforcement, they insisted, simply didn't work. In their hands, we could see how it wouldn't.

Nonetheless, we managed to scare employers and enforcers alike into taking their affirmative action responsibilities more seriously—though to be honest, on occasion we were the ones who were scared. One noontime, twenty of us crowded into the office of an affirmative action official high up in the Federal Building to urge him to carry out more vigorous enforcement of the regulations. The target official listened as our spokeswoman delivered her prepared statement. Then he came out from behind his desk and prowled back and forth while looking menacingly into our faces. "All right now!" he boomed in a deep bass voice. "How about if we hear from some of you less vocal ladies." Hearts began to pound, and there was a thud as Pat Cronin, a new member, fell to the floor. As the organizer, I sprang into action, hurrying to her side and lifting her feet to increase oxygen flow to her brain. She quickly came to, but the meeting was over.

Pat later became the chairwoman of 9 to 5, a position that required her to run meetings, speak at press conferences, and address large audiences. She often began her presentations by telling the story of how at her first "action" she'd been so terrified that she blacked out. If she could overcome her fears, she said, so could others.

———————

As the 1970s progressed, a cry of "reverse discrimination" arose, and affirmative action programs were challenged in the courts. The claim was that

White men were suffering as women and people of color were hired and promoted over them. In fact, figures show that during the 1970s, women and members of minority groups were indeed hired by federal contractors at a greater rate than by noncontractors. Yet there was little statistical evidence to suggest that White men were adversely affected. Again, some of the steps employers took to reverse the effects of past discrimination—being clear about job requirements during the hiring process, writing accurate job descriptions, posting job openings, expanding training programs, and creating career ladders—benefited *all* workers. Nonetheless, affirmative action regulations remained politically vulnerable. In the 1980s the Reagan administration cut back on enforcement of affirmative action. The gains made by women and people of color began to falter. And at the same time, Reagan attacked the rights of workers in general.

Pressing the government for stronger enforcement, embarrassing companies with "awards" for bad behavior, urging school boards not to buy from companies with discriminatory policies—these were all ways that the women of WIP pressed for change without having to confront their employers directly. And having warmed up with these approaches, they soon gained the courage to meet face-to-face with management.

At one venerable small press, employees and management held a series of meetings over the course of six months. They agreed on longer vacations, better life insurance, eight weeks of paid maternity leave and two weeks of paid paternity leave, a change in the overtime policy to bring it into compliance with state law, and a change in the "separation policy" to guarantee that professionals and nonprofessionals would be treated equally in cases of firing, resignation, or retirement.

A large textbook company dropped its blatantly discriminatory policy of charging women an extra seven dollars per month to include their spouses on their health insurance plan. (Men had been allowed to include their wives for free.)

In-house job posting became standard practice throughout the industry. Up to this point, rather than publicize job openings to employees, management at many companies preferred to advertise in the newspaper, recruit from an employment agency, or put the word out on some kind of informal grapevine. Some companies actually took deliberate steps to conceal job openings from employees. By the time women heard about the openings, they'd already been filled. But now, as women demanded change, one company after another began posting the openings. After a year of pressure, only one company—a highbrow national magazine—was still holding out.

The same thing happened with job training—another key element for fair treatment, not only for women but for all employees. We drew up proposals for change, sent groups of women to meet with management, and watched the changes roll in. We also issued a report on salaries, which showed that despite Boston's high cost of living, the average pay for publishing employees in the area lagged behind the national average. Shortly thereafter, one of the biggest companies awarded $200,000 in raises.

Traditionally, workers achieve job gains like these through unions. So far, we were managing to win change through intensive network building, surveying, public embarrassment, the strategic use of government enforcers—and the industry's *fear* of unions. And in fact, union drives would soon begin at two Boston-area publishing companies.

Meanwhile, the discrimination charges were still in the works. After five months, Attorney General Bellotti got in touch to say that he'd completed his investigation and was ready to move forward. Just before Thanksgiving in 1975, we called a meeting to announce his findings. (By this time, we'd progressed from "gatherings" to "meetings.") Once again, the church basement was packed. The suspense was palpable as Nancy Farrell, the new WIP chair, approached the podium. There was a hush as she declared that Bellotti had found evidence of race and sex discrimination at three of the largest publishing companies and had located the plaintiffs he needed in order to move forward. He was now prepared to file joint charges with 9 to 5, at both the state and federal levels, against Addison-Wesley, Allyn & Bacon, and Houghton Mifflin.

The room exploded with cheers and applause. I saw tears streaming down women's faces, and I felt myself choking up too.

A few days later we called a joint press conference with Bellotti at the State House. Every local TV station showed up, along with the *Globe*, the *Wall Street Journal*, and the publishing trade press. The next day, we blanketed the industry with leaflets saying it wasn't too late for more plaintiffs to come forward with additional evidence—not only about the three named companies but about any publishing company. The entire industry was on notice.

Massachusetts Attorney General Bellotti helped us press for fair treatment on the job. *Schlesinger Library, Harvard Radcliffe Institute; photo by Nicole Symons*

Not long after that, the three companies began settling the charges to the tune of a million and a half dollars, plus promises of new promotion and training policies. Hundreds of women received back pay, and employees across the industry—not just at the companies that had been sued—saw their salaries go up.

None of the companies admitted they'd done anything wrong. In fact, one CEO was at pains to protest the very idea that his company would even dream of treating women unfairly. "We think a lot of women," he earnestly assured the *Wall Street Journal*. "We think they're very nice." You can imagine how that earnest statement went over with WIP members.

Together, the women of WIP achieved more than anyone had foreseen. Hesitant at first, they'd followed their own judgment about how to move forward. They were persistent and they were bold. They learned that getting together to push for change could win results. Thanks to their courage and hard work, Boston's publishing industry was transformed. Now, throughout the industry, women were increasingly valued for their talents, their ideas, their contributions. It was no longer worth an extra

$3,500 to be a man in publishing, as it had been when we issued our first report. Pay and working conditions improved for *all* employees, male and female, White and of color.

My fear that the publishing women would be too timid and too easily co-opted turned out to be all wrong. So did my fear that they would intimidate other 9 to 5 members. The publishing women learned from the actions of 9 to 5'ers in other industries, and in turn they inspired others across the office world. The strategies they pioneered paved the way for bold action throughout the city.

Like the women of WIP, and like the publishing industry itself, I, too, was transformed. As I accompanied the publishing women on their adventure, I grew as an organizer. I got better at knowing when to push and when to back off. I gained more trust in my own judgment and in that of the women I was working with.

And now we were ready for the next challenge: starting a union.

9

A UNION OF WOMEN,
BY WOMEN, FOR WOMEN

A FEW MONTHS AFTER WE LAUNCHED OUR ORGANIZATION, Karen had an astrologer do her chart. She received an elaborate hand-lettered document predicting that her life would be filled with stout, balding men wearing pinky rings. The meaning of this forecast became clear when we started looking for a union that women office workers could join.

In our first two years, 9 to 5 had won more job improvements on an ad hoc basis than we had ever imagined possible. But right from the start, we felt certain that unions would be at least part of the solution for women's problems in the office. Clerical workers who were members of a union were clearly better off: they earned an average of 32 percent more and had more say over their work lives.

Companies that made changes in response to pressure from 9 to 5 could backslide whenever they chose. With a union contract, on the other hand, they'd be legally bound to keep their word. With a union, the employer was required by law to sit down and bargain over pay, benefits, and working conditions. Only with a union, we believed, could you truly "alter the relations of power," as my teachers at the Midwest Academy had put it. Besides, we weren't going to keep our scrappy, high-intensity independent organization up and running forever, were we? It was time to move to the next level—a more stable, more sustainable level.

And so, in 1975, two years after we started 9 to 5, we got to work making a union option available to our members. As usual we were thinking big. Women office workers would be the next great wave to demand their due. Not just that—when we did organize, we'd transform the labor movement all across America.

It had to happen! All the stars were aligned.

The prospect of deepening our ties with the organized labor movement thrilled me. My interest in unions went back to the stories I'd heard from my grandfather, the one we called Little Grandpa because he was barely five feet tall. (The other one, over six feet, was Big Grandpa.) After arriving on American shores from Lithuania early in the twentieth century, he'd attended rallies in New York's Union Square and listened to speeches by Rose Schneiderman, a leader of the Uprising of the 20,000, the massive garment women's strike of 1909. Schneiderman was only four feet nine inches tall (even shorter than he was), with flaming red hair. She had left school at thirteen to help support her family and had become a riveting orator. It was she, it's said, who coined the phrase "bread and roses." "What the woman who labors wants," she said, "is the right to live, not simply exist—the right to life as the rich woman has the right to life, to sun and music and art. . . . The worker must have bread, but she must have roses, too."

I was inspired by my grandfather's tales, and inspired again when I learned about the autoworkers and steelworkers whose strikes in the 1930s ushered in a new era of worker power. At the 1963 March on Washington for Jobs and Freedom, I was captivated by the sea of autoworker caps and signs calling for an end to workplace discrimination. I knew that Dr. King had traveled to Memphis in April 1968 to support striking sanitation workers; it was there that he'd delivered his famous "I've Been to the Mountaintop" speech the night before he was assassinated. I was inspired, too, by how the United Farm Workers of America, led by Cesar Chavez and Dolores Huerta, used a high-profile consumer boycott to build their power.

In college, for my senior thesis, I studied an organization called the Women's Trade Union League, founded in Boston in 1903, which played an important role in the garment worker strikes of the time. The league not only nurtured the leadership of women like Rose Schneiderman but also sent wealthy women in fur coats onto the picket lines. When these society ladies got arrested, the press paid attention and the struggle became a public issue. Like 9 to 5, the WTUL operated outside of the official labor movement but alongside it.

Some 9 to 5'ers had grown up with more direct ties to unions than mine. Janet's mother was a teacher who belonged to a union, and her father, who played the viola in the Cleveland Orchestra, did too. Janet remembered sitting at the kitchen table making posters—YOU CAN'T RUN AN ORCHESTRA ON A STRING—when her dad went on strike. Years later, when her father died, the musicians who came to mourn him talked not about the music making but about the union activity they'd shared.

Gilda Turner's father had worked for the telephone company for nearly four decades, starting as a ditch digger the year she was born and then moving up. "It was probably because of the union," she said, "that he was able to have a job as a Black man and keep it that long."

Kim Cook remembered going to union Christmas parties with her mom, who worked in an electronics factory. Half the workers were women, but for many years all the union leaders were men. She was proud when her mother won a seat on the union executive board.

In the 9 to 5 office in 1974, we cheered when we heard that three thousand union women had gathered in Chicago to found the Coalition of Labor Union Women (CLUW), with the goal of organizing the unorganized, promoting affirmative action, and increasing women's participation as union members and leaders. This meeting followed the launch of the Coalition of Black Trade Unionists in 1972, with participation by men and women from thirty-seven different unions.

Nonetheless, we were under no illusions about the chasm that separated most women office workers from the labor movement. When we asked women at a 9 to 5 meeting to throw out words they associated with unions, this is what we heard:

Blue collar	Bureaucratic
Male	Scruffy
Dirty job	Against the Equal Rights Amendment
Hard-hat jobs	Ineffective

Reactionary	Rigid
Pro–Vietnam War	Strike
Rednecks	Not needed anymore
Corrupt	Sexist
Gangsters	Not for office workers
Autocratic	

These negative associations weren't all off base. Unions *were* concentrated in blue-collar industries, and many of them *had* turned conservative. Since the waves of organizing in the 1930s and '40s, many unions *had* devoted themselves to serving their existing members rather than seeking to organize new ones. Some unions were notorious for acting to keep women and people of color out of their ranks. In 1972 George Meany, the longtime president of the AFL-CIO (the federation to which most of America's unions belonged), was asked why the percentage of unionized workers was declining. "I don't know," he replied. "I don't care. . . . Why should we worry about organizing groups of people who do not appear to want to be organized? . . . The organized fellow is the fellow that counts."

Kim's mother's union, with its female members led by male officials, was typical. Women made up 20 percent of union members but held less than 5 percent of union offices. By the 2020s women and people of color would move into top positions at several of the nation's largest unions. But those days were still to come.

At first, as we tried to imagine how women office workers would connect to unions, we envisioned a simple scenario. Women who were ready to unionize their offices would come to us for help. We'd call up a union to run an organizing drive. The drive would be successful because that's what unions knew how to do. Then we'd help the newly unionized women to bargain for a contract and run for union office. Soon, however, that scenario came to seem unlikely. As our friend Frank, the veteran organizer, kept telling us, the notion that we would simply hand women over to a union and let the union take it from there—well, that wasn't going to work, not for the women, not for the union, not for us. We wanted our union to be of women, by women, and for women—women who'd been ignored for too long by employers and unions alike. We needed to join forces with an existing international union (unions are known as "international" because they comprise members from both the United States and Canada), but we wanted to make our own decisions. We wanted to hire our own organizers and run our own organizing drives. That meant we wanted a charter to create a brand-new local union, a new unit with its own staff and officers, to which we would recruit members. And we wanted funding to get the new local off the ground.

Was there a union on the face of the earth that would agree to such terms? We started making appointments. For some union officials, even agreeing to meet with us was a stretch, and it was easy to see why. Most of them had never remotely considered organizing women office workers. And we at 9 to 5 didn't seem like a particularly strong bet, as we had neither experience in the union movement nor any solid prospects for organizing drives.

Nonetheless, our passion and confidence knew no bounds. Our pitch went something like this:

> Women office workers occupy a central position in the new economy. We're the largest sector—twenty million strong—and the only sector that's growing. The women's and civil rights movements have raised expectations of equality and fair treatment throughout the land. Yet the promise of the 1960s has not been met in the 1970s. Unemployment is 10 percent; inflation is 12 percent. More families than ever need two or more incomes to get by. Discontent is rising. Unions are desperately needed. The time is ripe.
>
> 9 to 5 speaks to office workers in words they will listen to. We represent enormous potential. Take a chance on us.

Once again, as we had two years earlier, we made the rounds of unions in the Boston area, this time with a proposal in hand. Simply because of its name, the Office and Professional Employees International Union (OPEIU) sounded like the natural place to start. We knew that the American Federation of State, County, and Municipal Employees (AFSCME) was devoting major resources to organizing public workers, including tens of thousands of clericals. The Communications Workers of America (CWA) represented telephone workers across the country, and the American Federation of Teachers (AFT) represented school secretaries. A small union called District 65, based mostly in New York, was organizing in the publishing industry there and was talking about expanding into Boston. The Teamsters union, based mostly in the freight industry, had also shown interest in organizing clerical workers. And the Service Employees International Union (SEIU), having started out as an organization of janitors and doormen, had expanded its ranks to include many other kinds of workers and was engaged in vigorous organizing campaigns across the country.

This time around, no one said anything like "women think with their cunts," as the unforgettable union official had done two years earlier. But once again, most of the unions simply weren't set up to take us on in the way we had in mind. Many of the officials couldn't quite wrap their minds around what we were talking about.

"Office workers aren't interested in unions," we heard. "They're impossible to organize."

"We couldn't possibly do what you're proposing within our structure," said more than one official.

"You look like good organizers," said one. "We'll be happy to hire a couple of you to work in one of our drives."

"As soon as you have some members," said another, "come back and we'll think about putting up some money."

I took the train down from Boston to New York to meet with an official from one of the unions on our list. I'd dressed carefully in my ugly wool pants suit, and I was sweating as I made my way from Penn Station to an ancient building in Lower Manhattan. Inside I threaded my way through a warren of wooden desks to locate the official. I asked for our own charter, the right to hire our own organizers, and $51,700—the budget we'd painstakingly drawn up.

"How about $6,000?" he said.

I went back to Boston. Back to the drawing board.

In time it was SEIU that emerged as our most promising option. It was the seventh-largest union in the AFL-CIO, with 650,000 members. (In 2005 SEIU left the AFL-CIO, and in 2021, with close to two million workers, it was the second-largest union in the United States after the National Education Association.) A majority of SEIU's members were women, 35,000 of them office workers. Twenty percent of its executive board members were women—not as many as there should have been, but the second-highest percentage in the AFL-CIO. (In later years SEIU would elect a woman president and a racially diverse executive board.) Women leaders within the union promised to mentor us. And SEIU locals had more power to set their own course than in many other unions. All of this made the union attractive to us. A mutual courtship began, and after months of negotiations, led on our side by Karen, we received a charter and funding for three years.

Success! We'd found a home in the labor movement—our own woman-led entity within a strong and growing international union. We were over the moon. On a visit to my parents, I sat at the dining room table and flexed my biceps. "I'm a labor leader!" I crowed.

We decided to call the new entity Local 925, pronounced "nine-two-five," a deliberate play on "9 to 5." If people were confused, well, we welcomed the confusion. The two entities were sister organizations, each with its own distinct structure, staff, officers, and membership—but entwined, both aiming to bring women together for rights and respect.

As the director of the new union, Karen moved into an office at the Y upstairs from 9 to 5 and hired two staff members. Dorine Levasseur was a 9 to 5 member, a clerical worker from a local public college who'd impressed Karen at first sight with her pizzazz. Jackie Ruff had started a union drive at the newspaper where she worked as a graphic designer. The newspaper fired her and the drive failed, and when she then applied for a job at the union, she was turned down. "We would never hire a woman organizer," she was told. In Local 925 she found the spot she was looking for.

––––––––––––

The team was ready for action. Now, right away, the difference between 9 to 5 organizing and union organizing came into high relief. In 9 to 5 we had freedom and flexibility. We could dream up a campaign in any shape or form. People could join as individuals, and we could define "victory" in any number of ways. Union organizing was another story altogether. It was governed by strict laws, most notably the National Labor Relations Act of 1935. In the 1930s and '40s, the law had given a tremendous boost to organizing among many kinds of workers, though it excluded agricultural workers and domestic workers, many of them people of color. Over the next forty years, however, the law had been amended repeatedly, becoming increasingly tilted toward the interests of management.

According to the law, here's what has to happen for employees to bring in a union:

First, at least 30 percent of employees at the workplace in question must sign a card declaring their interest in belonging to a union. (Most unions won't move ahead with a drive until at least 50 percent have signed.) Then the union petitions the National Labor Relations Board for an election, and a date is set, usually ten to twenty weeks in the future. On the appointed date, the National Labor Relations Board sends officials to hold the election. When the votes are counted, there's no room for creative interpretation. Unlike with a 9 to 5 campaign, either the union wins or it loses.

If the union does win, the next step is formal bargaining with the employer over pay, benefits, and working conditions. Once an agreement is reached, the contract usually remains in force for two or three years, after which it's time for another round of bargaining.

Those are the basics—on paper, that is. But the orderly progression of steps spelled out in the law is only a best-case scenario. In our experience, it never happened that way.

Right from the start, we put our special 9 to 5 stamp on our union organizing. Just as we'd had to work hard a couple of years earlier to develop an appropriate vocabulary for talking to office workers about 9 to 5, now we had to find the right words for talking about our new union. Many of the standard terms were unfamiliar to most office workers. What was an authorization card? What was the AFL-CIO? What was a drive, a bargaining unit, a local, a steward?

Our union leaflets and brochures had a distinct 9 to 5 slant. ROSES ARE NOT ENOUGH, proclaimed a lavender sheet adorned with a drawing of a flower. Another flyer was designed to look like a pink memo pad: WHILE YOU WERE OUT, SEIU CALLED TO SEE YOU. PLEASE CALL. URGENT.

Echoing 9 to 5's Bill of Rights, our union flyers addressed not only pay and benefits but also discrimination in hiring, training, and promotion. We talked about respect, sexual harassment, the right to choose whether to do a boss's personal work, maternity benefits, and equal benefits with men.

For the previous two years, our 9 to 5 organizing had aimed to show office workers throughout the city that change was possible. We were making progress toward that goal. Still, among many office workers the notion of individual agency—"I can change things"—was weak, and the idea of collective agency—"*We* can change things"—was even weaker. To many, the prospect of sitting across the table to engage in formal negotiations with management was unimaginable. Employers, of course, were intent on keeping it that way. When women dared to speak up as a group, their bosses tended to respond like this:

> Why didn't you come to me with your problems? If I had only known, I would gladly have talked to you individually.

> These things are much better handled one by one. I was so disappointed when you came in here as a group.

> I was just about to do what you're asking for, but because you came here with your petition, now I won't. I never respond to pressure.

According to management, employees would do best to value their individuality and stay away from organization like the plague. But needless to say, managers themselves were organized. Within companies, heads of departments generally didn't try to work things out one-on-one—they weren't allowed to. "I'd gladly change the policy if it were up to me," women were told, "but unfortunately, it's up to Personnel." Employers belonged to the Chamber of Commerce, the Personnel Managers Association, the Business Roundtable, the National Association of Manufacturers, and more industry lobbying associations than you could count. Management believed wholeheartedly in acting collectively. Yet employees were expected to forgo the strength of organization and deal with job issues strictly as individuals.

We were at pains to combat this idea. If management was organized, we'd better be organized too. "Individuals make a difference . . ." said the front cover of one of our brochures. When you opened it up, the headline inside read: INDIVIDUALS WORKING TOGETHER MAKE A *BIGGER* DIFFER-ENCE. We quoted a woman who'd written to us: "When I found out I had been working a lot longer on my job than someone else, and they were making more money and doing exactly the same job, I had to do something. I tried over and over again, but they just wouldn't listen. We needed a union to make them listen. If you find out they don't respect you as an individual, you have to try something else."

Part of putting a 9 to 5 stamp on Local 925 meant making sure that our members "owned" the union. Everything revolved around that goal. Dorine remembered: "The important thing was to put control in the hands of the members. It was their work life, and it would be *their* contract, *their* organizing drive. It wasn't our job to run the thing. It was our job to help people understand how *they* could run the thing. That's my job—just to show the way. Now you take it. And I'll be there. But this is your way."

Building on what Women in Publishing had already achieved, our first union campaign got underway at a publishing company. It was a tiny company, with only five employees, and it operated like a family. When the boss agreed to recognize the union in the summer of 1975, it was a small victory, but we were beyond elated. We were on our way.

The election win turned out to be far from the end of the campaign. "Family" or no, the boss fired three of the five members, and contract negotiations reached an impasse. We responded with the kind of feisty tactics we'd honed in 9 to 5. On a Saturday morning when the company was holding a conference for a dozen clients at its little suburban office building, we showed up in the parking lot with a conga line, banging on pots and pans. We chanted "Unfair!" at the top of our lungs and sang a song written especially for the occasion.

Monday morning, Karen was served with a subpoena. Our protest had violated the labor laws, the company claimed, by putting pressure on the company's clients. The threat of a libel charge also hovered in the air. The charges were withdrawn, but it took us a year to get a contract.

The target of our next union drive was one of the three publishing companies Attorney General Bellotti had charged with discrimination. The charges were still pending in 1976 when Allyn & Bacon management suddenly slashed health benefits. Hundreds of employees were angry about the takeback, and doubly so when management wouldn't respond to their complaints. Bearing out the old adage "The boss is the best organizer," a union drive took off.

Nancy, the chair of Women in Publishing, was an Allyn & Bacon employee. She called a meeting in the cafeteria and started off by telling the attendees that they had to reveal either their salary or their weight. Everyone laughed, but when people did reveal their salaries, many who thought they'd been getting a special deal were shocked—and angry—to learn that they weren't.

"Are you embarrassed to reveal your salary because it's too low?" Nancy asked. "Isn't it management who should be embarrassed? Who benefits from keeping this information secret?"

Some women were ready to join the organizing drive right from the start, but others were concerned about what their husbands, their supervisors, or their bosses would think. Nancy respected how hard it could be to sign a union card or to vote yes and recognized that women would take more risks if they felt supported by someone they felt close to. Gently, she sought to persuade women that being nice wouldn't get them as far as being strong.

Within eight days, 50 percent of employees had signed cards expressing interest in a union—at which point the company brought in a law firm to run an antiunion campaign. One evening, Nancy's phone rang. It was one of the supervisors who sympathized with the union, calling to offer behind-the-scenes support. "Get a pencil," the supervisor said. "I'm going to tell you what the antiunion campaign is going to look like, one week at a time." Now Nancy and her team were a step ahead. They could tell employees what they were about to hear from management and counter every argument.

Would a union be an invasive third party—and male dominated besides?

"Unions are what the members make them," we said. "In bargaining a contract, it's the employees who decide what issues concern them and the employees who negotiate with the employer." Local 925's drives were led by employees who paid close personal attention to the views and concerns of their coworkers.

Would the union destroy the friendly atmosphere in the office?

"To make change, you'll have to apply pressure," we said. "Once you've unionized, though, your employer will have a new respect for the organized power your union represents, clearing the way for even better working relations."

Organizing is the professional thing to do, we emphasized. "A union contract can legally guarantee the higher pay you deserve professionally and the respect you are entitled to for the valuable contribution you make to business and the economy."

Would a union mean time clocks, rigid wage scales, and regimented working conditions?

No, in fact it could mean the opposite.

Would a union force people to go on strike?

"A strike can be called only by a vote of the affected members," we assured people. "Over 95 percent of all contracts in the United States are settled without strikes."

Would a union assess heavy dues and use them to line the pockets of union leaders?

In Local 925 dues were capped at 1 percent of employees' salaries, with a maximum of fifteen dollars a month. "Only a vote of the membership can change the amount of dues. Your dues money is spent on services for you. And, through a union, salaries and benefits are almost always improved."

On the day of the election in 1977, I stood among dozens of employees who assembled after work to watch the count. When the union was declared the winner, the room erupted in cheers.

Once we'd won the election, just like at the smaller publishing company, contract negotiations were far from easy. The first day of bargaining hinted at just how tough they would be. As our team—mostly women—sat down at the table, a union supporter remembered, one of the company lawyers looked around in bewilderment. "Where is everybody?"

he asked—echoing the student who'd once looked Karen in the eye and asked, "Isn't anybody here?"

One Sunday Jackie took me to church to pray for a favorable contract. It was a desperate measure. I hadn't been brought up to pray and didn't really know how to. Maybe it was Jackie's pleas, not mine, that reached the heavens. At any rate, in 1978 we finally did win our contract. At both the tiny publishing company and at Allyn & Bacon, the contracts were good ones, with substantial wage increases, improved job training, vacation, and sick leave, better health insurance and protections for pregnant employees, and a grievance procedure. "History in the making!" our newsletter proclaimed.

———————————

Meanwhile, thanks in part to the work we were doing and to efforts independent of ours, organizing was taking off at Boston-area colleges and universities.

The region was crawling with institutions of higher learning, some big, some small, some elite, some less so. There was Harvard, with its historic Yard secured by ornate iron gates, MIT with its no-frills industrial-style buildings, Boston University straddling busy Commonwealth Avenue, Boston College and Tufts University with their leafy out-of-town campuses, and dozens of others, both public and private.

Office work at universities had many perks. Rules were looser than in the banks and insurance companies downtown. University office workers could move around and talk to one another, come in late, and leave early. The dress code was informal. Often you could take courses for free. There was the satisfaction of being involved in educating a new generation or contributing to groundbreaking research. Employees could sometimes express their complaints—as Karen and I had done with Harvard's personnel director, the one with the trembling hands—without fear of being fired. On the other hand, Janet *had* been fired when she protested "speed-up" (management's demand for higher production without higher pay) at Harvard Business School.

A big downside was the pay, which was low—sometimes even lower than at the financial firms. At every one of the colleges we surveyed, clericals (mostly women) earned less than buildings and grounds employees (mostly men). And of course there was that feeling of invisibility—the "Isn't anybody here?" syndrome.

Within 9 to 5, college and university office workers were Karen's bailiwick. As she visited one campus after another, she had no trouble finding women eager to get together. Activity sprang up quickly on more than a dozen campuses.

At one small college, a union drive was sparked by incidents like these:

"One day a supervisor was typing his own letter. A dean walked by and commented, 'Boy, some people will stoop to anything.'"

And this one: "We were given a handbook that said if we had any problems, we should go to the personnel office. But there *was* no personnel office."

At a larger campus, 75 percent of the clerical workers signed a petition for "rights, respect, and 20 percent," meaning a 20 percent across-the-board raise. The college president refused to accept the petition but assured the group that a "job reclassification" was in the works. The new scheme was a disappointment, though, and as discontent rose, the administration took the unusual step of purchasing a copy of a film about 9 to 5 that had aired on public television and taking it around from department to department, showing it to the clerical workers and warning that 9 to 5 was a radical organization that they should stay away from. Instead, in the spring of 1977, employees started a union drive.

Then we hit a wall. Although many university administrations were accustomed to dealing with buildings and grounds worker unions, they were determined to avoid clerical unions. One after another, these supposedly liberal institutions put up stiff resistance to the demands of their office workers. Even the smallest institutions hired major union-busting "consultants" to run intensive antiunion campaigns.

One place where a union drive did succeed was among the library workers at Brandeis University, located not far outside Boston. A few years earlier, these employees had formed a staff association, which, like 9 to 5, had no formal power. Now they were ready for something stronger. After interviewing several unions, they settled on ours. We were brand new, with virtually no track record, but they felt they could trust us.

The Brandeis University administration said publicly that it hon-
ored the right of its library employees to choose to join or not to join a
union, but in fact the university's behavior was far from neutral. Management exerted intense pressure on supervisors, training them to deliver
an antiunion message and making sure they did so. Nevertheless, when
the election was held early in 1976, the union won overwhelmingly. The
employees elected a negotiating team and got down to work deciding
what to bargain for.

Even after the election, however, management continued to put up
fierce resistance. Week after week, negotiations went nowhere. Karen
invited me to attend one of the sessions. As I watched her and the
library workers making their presentations before the team of stone-
faced administration reps across the table, it was clear that the two sides
were miles apart. But alumni, students, and faculty came to the aid of
the union, voicing support from near and far. Picket lines sprang up at
alumni events in New York, Chicago, and Atlanta, with flyers that read
Union-Busting Isn't Kosher—a reference to the university's roots in
the Jewish community.

Nine months later, we finally had our contract.

In 1974 Boston University announced a new pay structure for office
workers—a so-called merit plan that abolished regular wage increases and
instead forced individual office workers to compete against one another
for a share of the pot. The new level of insecurity, along with the rock-
bottom wages, was the last straw. A group calling itself SCAMP—"Staff
Committee Against the Merit Plan"—arose and began circulating a petition among the 850-person office workforce.

When SCAMP members presented the petition to the personnel director, she said she couldn't accept it. If she did, she said, she would be
recognizing the group as a union. A light bulb went off.

Barbara Rahke, an active 9 to 5 member, recalled how her perspective was changing at the time. One weekend, she said, "I was somewhere
socially and somebody asked me what I did. I said I worked at Boston University, but I went through contortions, trying to say what I did
without saying I was a secretary. Finally I realized what was going on. I
am an office worker, I work my tail off, I produce work for all kinds of

professors, I am getting paid nothing, and not only am I not ashamed—I should be screaming it from the rafters!"

Barbara took the lead in setting up interviews with several unions. The group settled on District 65, the union that was organizing clerical workers in publishing and higher education and at bookstores and museums in New York.

When the union drive began, the university mounted a vicious counter-campaign, Barbara remembered. An antiunion consulting firm flew people in from Chicago, and after the union had filed the required number of cards with the NLRB, a full year passed while the university filed challenge after challenge, doing everything it could to delay the election. Even when the election finally did take place in 1978 and the union won, the university refused to accept the results. Months went by while the administration insisted that the election was invalid and should be held all over again.

In response the office workers took a deep breath and decided to go on strike. In April 1979, using a time-honored union tactic, they set up multiple picket lines to block delivery trucks from entering the campus. The university responded by hiring off-duty cops to police the picket lines. Arrests were made, toes run over. The drivers of trucks and vans couldn't have been more surprised to see women in high heels carrying picket signs, but in accordance with labor custom, they refused to cross the lines and turned their vehicles around.

The strike worked. At last the university recognized the union, and bargaining began. But even then the conflict wasn't over. It took a second strike in the fall of 1979 before the university agreed to sign the contract.

In an article in the *Wall Street Journal*, the head of the antiunion firm hired by BU boasted that he'd conducted a hundred campaigns and lost only two. One of the two was the drive at BU.

The BU union survived and thrived, and Barbara went on to organize office workers at other universities. In 1980 District 65 merged with the United Auto Workers. The union's successful drives among clerical workers led to organizing campaigns among other higher education employees, including graduate students, adjunct faculty, postdoctoral students, student workers, and even student athletes. In the decades to come, other unions joined in the effort to organize on campuses. University administrations put up strong resistance, but campus organizing continued to grow.

In 1989 Harvard University signed a contract with the Harvard Union of Clerical and Technical Workers, which represented thirty-four hundred clerical and technical employees. It had been a long process indeed. I remembered the meeting Karen and I had participated in in 1973, the one where our group of two dozen office workers had rehearsed for weeks before filing into the office of the personnel director and reading out our list of demands. After that there had been several union elections and multiple slogans, including the famous "We can't eat prestige." After the failure of several highly public campaigns, the union supporters, who by that time had affiliated with AFSCME, decided that the best strategy was to operate under the radar. No buttons, no leaflets, no signs. Instead, the organizing team went department by department, talking to each employee individually, leaving no trace of a paper trail. The administration had no written evidence to seize on, nothing to argue against. Only on the day of the election did the campus bloom with festive balloons and placards, and this time the drive succeeded.

Now, finally, the Harvard employees had their union. By that time, across the country, 70 percent of union campaigns among university clericals had concluded successfully.

Back in 1974 a reporter had asked Harvard's personnel director (the trembling one) why the university was so strenuously committed to resisting the demands of office employees. In response, he waxed poetic. "Harvard," he said, "is like an oyster. It is continually pelted with little irritants, like tiny grains of sand. Eventually, that which irritates it becomes pearls, but you must wait a while."

At long last, the irritants had become pearls.

10

SE-CRE-TA-REES, UNITE!

BY THE MID-1970S, we were known all over Boston. Women throughout the region knew about our activities, and many felt part of what we were doing. One woman told us that when she opened her desk drawer on her first day at a new job, she found a tidy pile of 9 to 5 flyers waiting for her. She joined right away. And one morning, as I sat on the bus on my way to a shift at a downtown T exit, I saw a woman nudge her seatmate. "Oh, look!" she said, pointing to the stack of newsletters on my lap. "There's that newsletter again. *I* read that." Her voice was full of pride, and I felt proud too.

Our organization had grown stronger internally. In the newsletter, our spokeswomen were identified by name, and all the articles were signed. Many of our members were thrilled to have their names in print. In fact, being public could be protective. Remember, the National Labor Relations Act made it illegal for employers to fire women for organizing—not just union organizing, but any kind of organizing. Some women figured that if their employers knew they were active in 9 to 5 they'd be less likely to fire them. This line of reasoning didn't hold water for all 9 to 5'ers—many still considered it too risky to go public—but it did for some.

We'd built an executive board composed of officers and representatives from publishing, banking, insurance, and several other industries. The board met once a month, the industry committees every other week. Together, we learned the art of running meetings and participating in them, a new skill for nearly all of us. Ahead of each meeting, a staff member would sit down with the chair to make a detailed plan. Who would present each agenda item? Who would be prepared to respond? "Democracy," per the Midwest Academy, "is having well-thought-out alternatives for the membership to choose between."

Every active member was expected to help raise money. Fundraising was one way you could tell if an organization like ours was real. Did people care enough about 9 to 5 to pay for it? Dues were five dollars a year. Women in Publishing held a book sale. We hosted an annual holiday party, which included a bake sale, an auction, and an ad book in which local businesses paid to be listed. "Ken's at Copley wishes you success!" "Richard Joseph: hairdresser to active 9 to 5 members." Our annual tag day and our summer door-to-door canvassing operation brought in funds.

But all these forms of "grassroots fundraising"—the kind that sought out many small donations—weren't nearly enough to sustain us. Unlike unions, whose membership dues provided a steady income, we were dependent on grants and donations from outside. Our $3,500 church grant had kept us going through the first year. After that we spent countless hours reaching out to other church organizations and foundations.

Some of our funders agreed wholeheartedly with what we were doing. Others had boards full of corporate executives who weren't one bit comfortable with our confrontational tactics but were willing to fund research and other tamer efforts. We hooked up with local colleges to provide job training to clerical workers; our part of the curriculum was to teach women to speak up for themselves. All of this helped keep the organization running.

Our core group of active members adored the organization, and it came to occupy a central place in their lives. Some became close friends. A group went on diets together. At one point, a few of the most active members put out a spoof newsletter called *5 to 9*. They wrote the articles, took the photos, laid it all out, and got it printed—in secret—and then released it to the staff and board. One article spoofed the staff's lunch-eating prowess and awarded "the coveted Heather Memorial Award, a bronzed piece of pie and a cup of coffee teetering precariously on a clenched fist." A photo showed one of the cochairs tied to a railroad track, gladly sacrificing her life for the organization.

One of our board members wrote a song to the tune of "Those Were the Days," the English version of a Russian ballad that was typically crooned with poignant nostalgia. Our version was feistier, and we belted it out at meetings:

> Se-cre-ta-REES, unite!
> Let's show them How we FIGHT
> For better pay, promotions, and respect . . .

The thrill of the chase, the battle against the corporate class, was what kept us all going. Here we were, a tiny, underresourced organization run by twentysomethings, yet we were in the news nearly every week, taking on the men at the top of the power structure and scaring the daylights out of them.

Many of the accounts I've read about the feminist movement abound with stories of personal attacks and painful splits. One memoir claims that "nothing in our women's movement was ever accomplished without severe emotional depletion and fractured personal relations." Our experience was different. As 9 to 5 grew, there were occasional conflicts and blowups, but for the most part we functioned as a team. We all cared obsessively about the same things. We could talk for hours about phone trees, leafleting techniques, to-do lists. We felt deeply accountable to one another and to our members, and we held ourselves to high standards.

Janet came up with an evaluation form covering basic organizing skills and work habits, and all of us on the staff filled it out:

1. Do you plan your day, your week? Do you stick to the plan? Does it work?
2. Are you going to enough lunches with new people? Do you go with a list of tasks in mind?
3. Do you work with members on skills? Far enough in advance to make it meaningful? Do you have follow-up discussions? Do they get a next assignment to test their ability again?
4. Before every meeting, do you work out a clear agenda with the chair?

5. Do you call everyone before meetings?
6. Are you prepared with clear tasks that are to come out of the meeting?
7. Do you follow up on those who didn't come? Those who did? Does the chair do this with you?
8. Are there enough action events coming out of the committee you work with?

I look at this questionnaire today, and even though it's totally on target, I must say I feel for all of us who filled it out. It set a high bar indeed—we were very hard on ourselves.

Just as we created diverse roles that played to the strengths of the diverse members of our organization, so, too, we made room for different organizing styles on the staff of our union and our nonunion wing alike. Karen tended to feel sure of where she was headed, and people were eager to follow her. As always I kept a close eye on how people were feeling and how the stragglers were doing. We made a good team. She'd throw out a proposal, I'd raise questions about it, and we'd move forward together.

As the 9 to 5 staff grew (including interns, we came to number six or eight, occupying a suite of tiny rooms), we needed a more formal structure, and in 1976, by vote of the board, I was appointed the staff director. I felt ready for the new position and proud to be running our weekly staff meetings. I met with each staffer individually to go over plans, goals, problems, results. I hired new people and oversaw their training. I dealt with an organizer who wasn't pulling her weight, an office manager who sulked. I fired one, kept another on. I managed the fundraising and worked with our elected chair to prepare for executive board meetings. Staff and members alike looked to me for direction. Maybe some were even a little afraid of me. Even so, our camaraderie flourished. On Friday afternoons we would knock off around 5:00 PM and head for a nearby restaurant. We'd fill our plates at the salad bar and talk and talk. We couldn't get enough of one another.

I was busy all day, every day. Jeff had become very busy too. One day he'd stopped by the office of a statewide consumer group that was just starting up and found himself being offered a job as a community organizer. It took him about a minute to ditch his career in health care and accept the position. His supervisor, an old friend from the antiwar movement who'd been trained at the Midwest Academy, was eager to have him, with two caveats: he'd need a haircut, and he'd have to leave his turquoise ring at home. When bored, he had a habit of taking the ring off and poking his tongue through the hole. The ring would have to go.

Like Karen, Jeff was a natural organizer. While it's true that the first meeting he called in the group's campaign for lower gas and electric rates drew exactly zero attendees, the new organization took off like wildfire, and within a few weeks, his wing of it did too. Drawing on churches and block associations, the group had no trouble finding people willing to speak publicly and could easily turn out hundreds or even thousands for a demonstration or a lobby day. The organization rented a whole floor for an office and hired dozens of staffers. Jeff was in the thick of it.

My job took up so much time and energy that I didn't have much left over for the group house I was living in. I wasn't much of a housemate. In the mornings, while others sat around the breakfast table companionably reading the newspaper, I would blow through the kitchen and grab something from the fridge before rushing out the door with my stack of leaflets. I rarely made it home for dinner. When I came in at eight or nine, I'd find the group talking or watching TV, and sometimes I'd join in, but just as often I'd head for my room, too tired to socialize. On weekends, Jeff came over and we mostly hung out in my room, not always quietly. I remember a time when one of my more severe housemates, the economist, banged on my door and asked us to tone it down. At the time Jeff was dancing on the bed wearing a T-shirt upside down, with his legs through the armholes, and I was swinging a nightgown overhead trying to make him lose his balance.

I didn't exactly neglect my chores, but I did the bare minimum—or maybe a little less. On Sundays, my night to cook, I'd show up in the kitchen at about 5:15 PM and try to come up with a last-minute dinner plan. Maybe I'd bake a quick corn bread, scramble a panful of eggs, and chop apples and oranges for a fruit salad. Or I'd throw leftovers in a pot with a little water, bring it to a boil, and call it soup. Then I'd take both dishwashing slots and be done for the week. After a while, I noticed that most of my housemates had taken to signing out whenever I was cooking.

With his new job at the consumer organization, Jeff was almost never around at his house either, and his roommates, who expected a deeper level of emotional involvement than mine did, were starting to get annoyed.

More to be free of our obligations to our housemates than out of a real desire to share a home with each other, we began making plans to move in together. We found an apartment near the high school in Somerville, a two-bedroom on the third floor, with the owners living downstairs. Perched on a hill, it had a view of the Boston skyline, including the John Hancock Tower. The apartment was cozy, and it turned out that we enjoyed being together without having to make a date. We didn't fight as much either.

In honor of Jeff's thirtieth birthday, I planted thirty little items (a pair of socks, a secondhand lamp, a memo pad) around the apartment and sent him on a scavenger hunt. He made me a bathrobe by sewing two orange-and-yellow towels together. We planted seedlings in old milk crates on the back porch, and by the end of the summer we'd succeeded in harvesting a carrot, a tomato, and an eggplant. In the winter the place was cold, and Jeff's mother sent me a kind of comforter that was like a sleeping bag with arms. In the evenings, after coming home from a meeting and getting something to eat, I'd zip myself in and settle on the couch with a book. Jeff's meetings ran later; often he didn't show up before 10:00 PM. Our furnishings were bare bones—no jewel colors or lush, deep-green plants like the ones I'd imagined up on my bluff on vacation. In truth, there wasn't much to our home life, but we didn't really want more.

———————

Not long after we moved into the apartment, an act of God sparked one of 9 to 5's most memorable skirmishes with the powers that be. On a Sunday in early February 1978, weather forecasters warned that a historic blizzard was on the way. Blizzard or no blizzard, first thing Monday morning I was out at the bus stop as usual. By the time I got to the office, the snow was falling so heavily that all I could see out the window was a blur of white. Inside the Y it was quiet and peaceful. Almost everyone else on the staff had been wise enough to stay home.

By early afternoon, my desk radio was reporting that employers had been instructed to send everyone home. Jackie, the one other staffer who'd been foolish enough to come to work, suggested it might be time for us to leave too. By now the T system had shut down. It took us several hours to plod through the Public Garden and the Boston Common, across the bridge over the Charles River, and up Mass Avenue toward home.

We were out of work for a week. Governor Mike Dukakis appeared on TV in a powder blue cardigan sweater and declared that no one was allowed downtown. Jeff and I made a pot of soup and padded around in thick socks. The men on our block spent every day under the blue sky in shirt sleeves shoveling out their cars. By the end of the week, we 9 to 5'ers were gliding over the drifts on cross-country skis and getting together at Karen's apartment to plot and scheme.

Monday morning, when people first started returning downtown, we were out in force at the T exits, standing in the drifts with our armloads of leaflets: "Is your company giving you a snow job?" The snow emergency had canceled work, but there'd been no cancellation of rent payments, food costs, or other bills. While executive salaries went untouched, we'd received calls from clerical workers who weren't being paid for the week that the city was shut down. We met with the secretary of economic development and demanded that employers be required to pay for the missed time. Any worker not paid for the snow week, we said, should be allowed to collect unemployment.

We requested a response by the end of the day, and indeed, the very next day found us issuing a press release applauding the governor's emergency bill providing that workers wouldn't lose pay because of the storm. The money came out of employers' pockets in the form of tax contributions to the state unemployment fund. The legislation passed, and hundreds of thousands of employees across the state were guaranteed a week's "snow pay."

11

IN OUR GLORY! (PART II):
THE WALLPAPER COMES ALIVE

THE CORE OF THE BOSTON ECONOMY was the finance industry—banking and insurance. We were ready for the big time.

The stories we heard from women in the finance industry were the worst of all. Full-time bank employees didn't make enough to qualify for a mortgage or a car loan. Some earned so little that they were eligible for food stamps. We heard from insurance workers who couldn't afford to get sick. A full-time office worker at the John Hancock insurance company told us she'd been forced to give up custody of her child when a judge ruled that her salary was too low.

Most of the workers in finance were women, and more than three-quarters of them held clerical jobs. Women held only a tiny percent of professional and sales jobs. In banking, profits were increasing by annual rates of 27 percent or more, but pay for women hovered close to minimum wage. Just like in publishing, although Boston's cost of living was *higher* than the national average, banks paid their clericals *less* than the national average.

The stories kept coming. When Diane, a bank secretary, asked for a raise, her boss suggested she see a psychiatrist. Fran applied for a promotion from clerk to underwriter. "Give me a chance," she implored. In response, her boss handed her a manual as thick as a telephone book and told her to come back when she'd finished reading it. She did read the book, but she never got the promotion. Gail had worked at her bank for eleven years and was the sole support of an eight-year-old daughter. She bid on a job opening, but the position went to a recently hired nineteen-year-old man. "He has a new house and a wife to support," she was told. Sandy was a lower-level bank officer. A young man was hired after her, and she was asked to train him. Now he was earning almost $5,000 more per year.

As the economy transitioned from an industrial to a service base, finance had become the biggest business, both in Boston and in the nation. Banks and insurance companies had the assets, the expanding workforce, and the influence to take the lead in implementing enlightened employment policies. They weren't doing so. The problems were as clear as day. The solutions were obvious. The question was how to make it happen.

We created a leaflet that showed a stick of dynamite protruding from a stylish platform shoe, with the headline WOMEN IN INSURANCE: AN EXPLOSIVE SITUATION, and we passed out six thousand of them announcing an event at the Y. I actually did my leafleting wearing a pair of platform shoes, in which I could barely walk. At least once a day, an ankle gave way with a sickening crunch. I wore them anyway. They made me feel very tall. Janet wore platform shoes too, and one day on her way to a recruitment lunch in a bank cafeteria, one of the heels collapsed. She hobbled to a seat, greeted her lunch date, and made some excuse not to stand up at the end of the hour. Somehow she made her way back to the office.

In the publishing industry, you could call a meeting and watch the room fill to bursting. Not in finance. Despite our clever leaflet and our hours of phone calling, our insurance event was a bust. Only fifty-five women showed up, including a generous sprinkling of company spies, who stood out with their nervous glances and frenzied note-taking.

It wasn't a matter of proximity. The John Hancock insurance company, with its six thousand employees, was located just a few steps from the Y. Liberty Mutual, with another few thousand employees, was five minutes away. Getting to the meeting couldn't have been easier. So where was everybody?

We went to Ken's to figure out what to do. Janet ordered her usual—a poached egg "in a cup, please, not on the plate"—and took the lead in

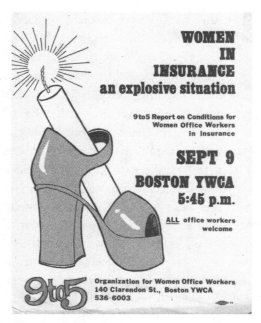

The stick of dynamite in the platform shoe said it all. *Author's collection*

the discussion. Having met with countless women in finance, she was not really surprised, she said, that so few people had shown up at our event. The barriers to organizing were huge. The industry's culture was so authoritarian that supervisors grabbed our leaflets right out of women's hands as they came in the door and explicitly warned them not to attend our meetings. Much of the workforce was very young. In fact, recruiters from insurance companies were invited into Boston's public high schools to sign up graduating seniors (girls, that is) for entry-level clerical jobs.

We would have to live with the reality, Janet said, that with occasional exceptions, women who worked in banks and insurance companies would not come to 9 to 5 meetings, hand out leaflets, speak at press conferences, or meet with their bosses. We'd have to devise a way forward that took those limitations into account.

The strategy we came up with had three elements.

Element no. 1 was government pressure. Just like in the publishing industry, a charge or a lawsuit wouldn't create change in and of itself, but in combination with other elements, it could be a powerful tool. We made a systematic study of all the government entities that might be of use. The most obvious choice was the Massachusetts Commission Against Discrimination, but we stayed away from it. We knew that officials there would be waiting for us with a stack of special forms to fill out—forms that could be filed away and never seen again. We kept digging, and in time we unearthed an obscure executive order that allowed the state insurance commissioner to regulate employment policies. According to this order, an insurance company that discriminated could be denied a license to do business. In fact, the entire industry could be denied a rate increase if enough companies refused to change their ways.

The order had never been used, but our new governor, Mike Dukakis, had just appointed a new insurance commissioner. Jim Stone was a twenty-seven-year-old wunderkind who was rumored to have cut his hair by about five inches when he got the job. Freshly shorn and dressed in a suit, he looked like a kid in grown-up clothing. In the spring of 1975, we brought a few dozen women to his office at lunchtime, showed him the executive order, and urged him to use it to bring the insurance companies of Massachusetts into line.

OK, he said.

He asked us to send a group of members to work with him on drafting standards for fair employment in the insurance industry. What they came up with was a close approximation of the Bill of Rights for Women Office Workers that we'd created and unveiled at our hearing. The standards included unisex job application forms, written job descriptions, job posting, posted pay scales guaranteeing equal pay for men and women in the same job, no more dead-end jobs, new bridge jobs to create career ladders, and equal benefit plans for men and women.

Stone issued the new standards for public comment and scheduled two hearings to listen to testimony. Bosses showed up in droves to testify that the new regs were unnecessary. Discrimination was already prohibited by state and federal laws, they said. The regulations would discriminate against men, they claimed. Employment policies were a private matter outside the purview of the commissioner, they maintained.

We testified too. Discrimination was not a management prerogative, we argued. The Massachusetts Commission Against Discrimination, the secretary of consumer affairs, and the governor backed us up. So did

Stone himself. He signed the new regulations—the first of their kind in the nation—and the day they arrived in the mail at the 9 to 5 office, screams of joy filled the air.

Immediately, however, two insurance companies challenged the regulations in court and won an injunction. The new regs were moved to the "speedy trial list," and there they sat.

But government pressure was only part of our three-pronged strategy. Now for element no. 2: creating safe ways for women workers to make their voices heard. Given that women in finance were unlikely to feel comfortable speaking up publicly, either inside or outside their companies, we looked for other things they could do. We hit on the idea of getting women to feed us information—to act as "whistleblowers," you could say. As soon as the new regulations were signed, we leafleted all the major insurance companies with a "scorecard" for employees to fill out and mail to us anonymously. How well does your company adhere to the new standards? Does your company have job descriptions, job posting, job training? We slapped the survey results onto a flyer tailored to each company, along with the anecdotes that had come our way, and leafleted again.

An advantage of the anonymity was that management didn't know who they were dealing with. Who was it who had leaked the latest pay scales? Was it that quiet receptionist in the executive suite? What were those women in the typing pool whispering about during coffee breaks? Could they be talking about a union? If bosses were used to thinking of their clerical workers as "wallpaper," as Janet had described it, now the wallpaper began to come alive.

The campaign began to bear fruit. One day an envelope arrived in the mail with no return address. Inside was a copy of a letter that the president of New England Life had circulated to his management team, saying that NEL intended to comply with the "substance of the personnel practices and policies the commissioner is advocating." Although the new regs were stalled in court, the companies knew that change was afoot. This company, for one, decided to get ahead of the curve.

Element no. 3 was public embarrassment. The finance industry was huge, wealthy, and powerful—much bigger and more powerful than the publishing industry—but it had its vulnerabilities. Both banks and insurance companies had an Achilles' heel: for them, image was everything.

Public confidence was their lifeblood. Simply bringing women's grievances into public view would take us a long way.

We got good press coverage in June 1977 when we picketed a convention of eight hundred bankers, waving signs and singing a takeoff on an old protest song called "Banks of Marble":

> I've been around this city
> Worked at lots of banking jobs
> And I've never seen a holdup
> but I know that we've been robbed!
>
> Oh, the banks are made of marble
> Women work on every floor
> And it's time we got together
> That's what 9 to 5 is for!

We got press coverage again when we coaxed the banking commissioner, Carol Greenwald, to conduct a survey of pay in the banking industry and hold public hearings on discrimination. In 1978 her investigation revealed that statewide, of the 258 employees in the top 5 percent of the salary range, only three were women. Of all women working in the banking industry, fewer than 5 percent were Black. The press covered us yet again when we visited the state treasurer, Robert Q. Crane, and urged him to take employment practices into account in deciding which banks would be eligible to participate in a new loan program.

We also released our own wage survey of several dozen insurance companies. Pay for Boston's insurance women, we found, lagged behind pay in other cities and also behind that of male coworkers doing comparable work. In response one company issued a statement saying that it did not discriminate and accused 9 to 5 of entering its building illegally (possibly true). Another company told the news media that our survey was "invalid."

Then three major insurance companies announced raises worth several million dollars.

———

So far we'd targeted the insurance and banking industries as a whole, on a citywide scale. What would happen if we picked out one particular company and went after it alone?

New England Merchants Bank was our first test case. Having received numerous calls from employees about equal pay violations there, we pressured federal affirmative action enforcers to investigate, and when they did, they uncovered a large group entitled to back pay. New England Merchants was a prominent sponsor of the Longwood Tennis Tournament, and in August 1977 we showed up at the games carrying signs in the shape of tennis rackets that read, EVEN THE SCORE FOR WORKING WOMEN! We then went back to State Treasurer Crane, who declared that because of the pay violations, he would be withdrawing state money from the bank. Bingo! We earned a big newspaper headline, and job conditions at the bank began to change at last. Women got promoted, and pay went up.

The pressure on New England Merchants had a broader effect too. No one, we found, acts faster than the company next door, the one that

We demonstrated at Boston banks. *Nancy Farrell*

is *not* being targeted. While we kept up the pressure on NEM, five other banks started posting jobs. Two beefed up their training programs. After we passed out a leaflet in front of State Street Bank, office workers there got a 5 percent raise. Another bank agreed to meet with a group of our members to discuss how to improve job conditions. It didn't matter that the women who worked at that bank weren't willing to be public at the meeting. They gave us advice behind the scenes, and members who worked at other banks took the speaking roles.

We were making progress. Our three-part strategy—using government pressure, creating safe ways for women to make their voices heard, and embarrassing the companies publicly—was working. What would happen if we aimed even higher?

———————————

As the biggest bank in town, the First National Bank of Boston was the industry leader. With fifty-three hundred employees and a thirty-seven-story tower on Federal Street, it was the second-largest employer in Boston, outstripped only by the John Hancock insurance company. Being the big cheese was worth a lot in public image, but paradoxically, it also made the bank vulnerable. Other banks, we surmised, probably hated the First for being number one. And as a symbol, it attracted plenty of attention, which we could use to our advantage.

The bank was already under fire. Attorney General Bellotti was suing the bank for illegal lobbying. A community group had accused the bank of multiple offenses: illegal redlining in its lending practices, encouraging Massachusetts businesses to move out of state, and supporting the South African system of racial apartheid.

We launched our campaign against the First on National Secretaries Day in 1979. Our opening move was to send two staffers to deliver a "Bad Boss Award" to the bank's CEO. They didn't expect to get past the front desk, but to their amazement they were sent upstairs. A secretary ushered them into the office of the CEO, who was waiting with an associate. As our staffers solemnly unscrolled a proclamation and read it aloud, everyone struggled to keep a straight face. Once back in the elevator, the staffers collapsed in giggles. Possibly the two managers did too.

That evening we publicly announced the campaign at a meeting at Faneuil Hall. The newly refurbished historic venue on the waterfront had been the site of impassioned oratory for more than two centuries. Before the founding of the American republic, the cry of "No taxation without representation!" had echoed off its walls. George Washington and Susan B. Anthony had spoken from the podium. Now Pat, our chair (the one who'd fainted during the meeting with the federal official) stood on the same dais and declared 1979 the "Year of the First." "The First sets the pace for employment policies throughout the city," she said. "When the First meets our demands, women in offices all over the city will benefit."

When a *Globe* reporter called the bank for a reaction, a spokesman stated that pay scales at the First were competitive with other businesses. That was exactly the problem! The First should have been leading the way in paying decent salaries. Instead, the bank seemed to be leading a race to the bottom. The bank's own affirmative action plan showed that women were "underutilized" in fifteen of thirty-six job categories. One simple way to address this problem would be to make sure all employees, not just a select few, heard about job openings. The year before, we'd met with the First's affirmative action officer to urge him to start posting jobs. He'd refused, insisting that the existing system of having employees "keep their eyes and ears open" was better. Job posting, he said, would be bad for morale. Imagine how disappointed employees would be if they heard about an opening but didn't get the job.

Now that our campaign had been announced, however, management changed its mind. A bank spokesperson announced that job posting would begin in six weeks. First victory at the First!

We rushed out a leaflet congratulating the bank for making progress and distributed it at lunchtime outside the building. Along with the congratulations, we opened an anonymous hotline exclusively for First employees. The line immediately began ringing off the hook. Tips poured in about problems employees were upset about.

We heard about the time a man and a woman applied for the same job. The man had a college degree. The woman had several years of experience and had taken banking courses. The man got the job "because of the degree," said the supervisor.

Another time, a man and a woman applied for the same job. The woman had a college degree. The man had taken banking courses. The man got the job—"because of the banking courses," said the supervisor.

Women in their fifties who were longtime supervisors and wanted to advance to officer status were told they couldn't apply, we heard. "Every time a management trainee comes through, it's someone from outside," our informant said. "This is the big gap at the First."

All these stories appeared in the first issue of *First People First,* our new newsletter for employees at the bank. The second issue took up the matter of pay:

Richard Hill [the bank's chairman] earns as much money in one day as clerical workers earn in a month.

First earnings rose 33 percent over the previous year. How much did your salary rise?

Within days, rumors of an across-the-board raise began circulating within the bank.

We doubled down on the pressure. We testified before the US Senate Banking Committee in Washington, DC, noting that a total of only thirty-five government employees were responsible for enforcing federal antidiscrimination regulations at 19,000 banking institutions nationwide. Only 2 percent of banks had ever been reviewed, leaving 18,620 banks free to discriminate.

At the behest of the Senate committee, banking became a special target of federal enforcement. When we called for an investigation of the First, the bank resisted by refusing to release its affirmative action plan, even though it was required to do so. The feds pushed ahead, announcing that officials would soon arrive on-site to gather information. We lost no time in recruiting women to speak confidentially with the investigators.

When summer came, we dispatched a team of college students to stand outside the bank's numerous branches and gather signatures from depositors who pledged to switch their accounts to another bank unless job conditions improved. We invited churches, unions, and other organizations with accounts at the First to join a "shadow board" that would monitor the bank's progress toward fair employment. We demonstrated outside the annual stockholders' meeting. We asked mayoral candidates to pledge not to invest city funds at the bank until changes were made.

By the end of the "Year of the First," our early job posting victory had been followed by many others. Fifty-one women had been promoted to officer jobs. Training opportunities and vacation time had been expanded. And employees had been awarded raises of up to 12 percent, the largest increase in the bank's history.

By December 1980, it was time to take on our next target. Our number one nemesis, the John Hancock Mutual Life Insurance Company, loomed just outside our windows at the Y. I was still carrying my shard of John Hancock glass in my purse, but the days of the defective windows were over. The company had spent a reported $7 million to replace the panes. Now the tower soared sky blue and magnificent into the heavens, but inside, the situation was far from pretty.

The Hancock was the largest private employer in Boston and the fifth-largest insurance company in the world. Of its six thousand employees, four thousand were women. More than 85 percent of the lowest-level jobs were filled by women. There were only six women executives, and none of them were people of color. Entry-level pay for file clerks and typists was at the bottom of the barrel. We issued a call for a 10 percent raise for all nonmanagement employees, full job posting (currently only lower-level job openings were posted), expanded training and promotion opportunities, and funding for day care for children of employees. Early on at 9 to 5, we'd considered employer-funded day care a utopian goal. Now we were ready to demand it.

Years later Karen served on a panel with a high-level executive from the Hancock who said that on the day we announced our campaign he'd barricaded himself in his office and slept there all night. It was unclear why he thought that guarding his office in this way would help, but he was right to perceive that the battle was on. Using the formula that had worked so well at the First National Bank, we pulled out all the stops.

We taped leaflets inside the stalls in the ladies' rooms. We set up a hotline and reported what we were hearing in a newsletter called *The Hancock Observatory*. A full one-third of respondents to the survey we passed out said they'd trained men to be their supervisors. Women were scarce in high-level jobs, we learned; to hear our informants tell it, "men [were] usually hired into higher-level jobs, regardless of experience."

"I was asked to replace my boss," one woman wrote. "He was earning three times my salary, but I received no promotion or salary increase."

On National Secretaries Day in 1981, we asked for a meeting with the chairman of the board. He demurred, saying that such a meeting "would not serve any useful purpose." We left a thousand postcards in support of our demands in the lobby.

We released a list of twenty-one organizations, churches, and unions that were endorsing our demands. Local unions that had invested their pension funds in the company wrote to Hancock management in support of our campaign.

By the end of a year of pressure, we'd won an impressive list of improvements in working conditions. Management signed an agreement with federal affirmative action officials promising to increase hiring and promotion of women and people of color. The company set up a committee to develop career paths for all levels of employees and created a "complaint review process"—similar to what is known in union contracts as a grievance procedure. And the company announced that through the United Way, it would be donating $100,000 to three community childcare centers.

Finally, the company increased starting salaries for clericals by fifteen dollars a week and announced an across-the-board pay raise of 10.5 percent. As with the First National Bank, it was the largest increase in company history—and more than what we'd asked for.

A word about the raises: early on, we assumed that management everywhere would be fierce about hanging on to every last penny. The last thing employers would be willing to give, we believed, would be money. But like many of our assumptions, that one turned out to be wrong. Along with concessions on job posting, job descriptions, job training, and promotions, the companies could readily afford to give raises, and they did. In fact, sometimes it was easier for them to reach into their pockets and share some of the wealth than to make other changes in how they ran their businesses.

We went after the problem of low pay in another way too. Early on, we discovered the existence of a shadowy organization of three dozen major employers called the Boston Survey Group. Since 1956 the group had been getting together regularly to share data about clerical wages and benefits. On National Secretaries Day in 1980, we filed a complaint with Attorney General Bellotti charging the group with conspiracy under the Sherman Antitrust Act.

Everyone knows that price-fixing—when competing firms get together and decide what to charge consumers for their goods—is illegal. It turns out that wage-fixing is illegal too. The official term is *monopsony*. Competitors are not allowed to meet to discuss wages in order to keep them low. Despite the Boston Survey Group's innocuous-sounding name, we charged that its actual purpose was not simply to *survey* wages but in fact to collude in keeping them low. The free market is supposed to follow the laws of supply and demand. If the supply of clerical workers is inadequate to meet the demand, then wages are supposed to go up. Yet even though there was a reported shortage of office workers in Boston, clerical wages remained shockingly low. The Boston Survey Group, we believed, was part of the reason why.

"Management tells you not to talk about your salary with coworkers," our spokeswoman said at the press conference where we announced the filing of our complaint, "but meanwhile they're meeting with their competitors to discuss your pay." While employers claimed that salaries were an individual matter between a woman and her boss, they were busy sharing information about salaries with every personnel manager in town.

We trotted out a list of statistics:

- Boston's cost of living is the highest in the country.
- Of the fifteen largest American cities, pay for Boston's women office workers is the third lowest.

- Top executives' base salaries rose nearly 20 percent over the past two years. Meanwhile, raises for clerk-typists averaged only 3.1 percent in 1979, and only 5 percent for executive secretaries.
- For every dollar earned by top executives, the average woman office worker earns only three cents.

The group's membership included representatives from virtually every industry in Massachusetts. Instead of bidding for workers by offering competitive pay, we charged, they were artificially preventing pay from rising and falling by "fixing" clerical wages. Suspiciously, members were sworn to secrecy about what the group was up to.

When the media called the group and asked for a response, a spokeswoman claimed, improbably, that the group actually functioned to *increase* pay for women office workers. As a spokesperson for the John Hancock insurance company put it, the group "acts to raise wages by keeping companies informed, so that they can move more quickly . . . in order to stay competitive."

The group declined to disclose the names of its members or any details about what kind of information was exchanged at meetings. That information, a spokesperson said, was confidential and had to be kept under wraps "purely for the protection of employees."

But confidentiality was a tricky thing when women were scheduling the group's meetings, typing the agendas, booking the venues, and sending out the minutes. Once the news about our charge appeared in the press, women began getting in touch and telling us what they knew. Soon we were in on when and where the group was meeting and who would be in attendance, and we began showing up outside the meeting places with signs and slogans. When we found out that the Federal Reserve Bank—a public entity—belonged to the group, we approached not only the bank's Board of Governors but also the House and Senate banking subcommittees in Washington, DC, and called for an investigation.

It took Attorney General Bellotti two and a half years, but in August 1982 he announced that he and the Boston Survey Group had reached an agreement. While admitting no guilt, the group agreed to publish a list of its participating members; to collect wage data only in the aggregate, not job by job and category by category; and to make the data public—all of which made it far more difficult for the group to pursue nefarious aims.

The agreement made national news and set a precedent for similar groups that were operating in San Francisco, Pittsburgh, Hartford, and elsewhere.

Once again, we declared victory.

———————————

I don't remember what happened to Commissioner Stone's insurance regulations. Either they were thrown out for good or they remained on the "speedy trial list" for all time. It didn't matter. Our multifaceted strategy of government pressure, anonymous "whistleblower" information, and public embarrassment had proved to be a stunningly effective formula.

Now we were determined to test that formula on a bigger scale. It was time to go national.

12

GOING NATIONAL

IN BOSTON, EVEN WITHOUT A MASSIVE MEMBERSHIP BASE, and without being a union, we were accomplishing more than we'd ever imagined. We'd forced the most powerful corporations to change their ways. For every company that we targeted specifically, many more scrambled to clean up their act. For every individual woman who took part in our meetings, forums, hearings, and demonstrations, many more watched and listened and were moved and changed.

Since the beginning we'd been hearing from women all over the United States, always with the same concerns: low pay, men earning more, few opportunities for advancement, a lack of everyday respect. Women everywhere believed they deserved better:

> I love my job. I just want to get paid decently and feel like I can get somewhere.

> The work itself is exciting because every day presents a new challenge. But I can't work under these conditions much longer.

> I literally couldn't believe it when I learned women earn only fifty-nine cents for every dollar a man makes. I can see with my own eyes that the women in my office are actually doing the lion's share of the work.

I am qualified enough and ambitious enough. I want to get paid enough to enjoy some things in life.

You're expected to have the right attitude, the right wardrobe, the right skin color.

There's no freedom of speech, no freedom of assembly. We give up our Bill of Rights for $115 a week.

And they were ready for action:

All my life I've been giving to other people—my husband, my children, the church. Now it's time for me to do something for myself.

Being Black, female, and a single parent, I think the most important thing working women can do is work together.

I feel that women working together can move mountains. 9 to 5 gives me the hope that things will be different for my daughter.

Starting in 1976, five working women's organizations from across the country—9 to 5 in Boston, New York Women Office Workers, San Francisco Women Organized for Employment, Cleveland Women Working, and Dayton Women Working—had begun meeting regularly to share research and strategies.

Now, with a sense of great excitement, we began to explore the possibility of expanding to more cities and founding a full-fledged national organization.

Karen took the lead in developing our expansion model. When calls came in from the small cities not far from Boston, she'd follow up, offering a simple formula for starting a local organization. Put out the word through the YWCA, the local women's center, the women's studies department at the local college, she advised, and then set a date for a small meeting. Karen would then arrive in town carrying a stack of leaflets headlined WORKING WOMEN IN WORCESTER, say, full of statistics from the Department of Labor. The pattern of discrimination and low pay was the same everywhere.

Meetings were places to strategize, listen, speak up, and vote. *Richard Bermack*

Together, Karen and the small local group would plan out a few further steps—research, a survey, targeting one or more employers—and schedule a first public meeting. Then it was on to the next city. She traveled throughout New England, leaving new chapters in her wake, then moved on to New York State: Albany, Rochester, Syracuse. The formula worked nearly everywhere. We added chapter after chapter to our roster.

Karen's boyfriend had moved to Cleveland, and in 1977 she made plans to join him. Cleveland Women Working, our organization in that city, was one of our most dynamic branches. She could move into the office there and open our national headquarters in the heart of the Midwest.

It all made sense, but as the date of her departure drew near, I felt dread in the pit of my stomach. How could she be leaving me?

The night of her goodbye party, I almost couldn't go. I showed up late, and when I walked in and spotted her across the room, my throat choked with tears. I buried my face in her shoulder and sobbed.

Such displays of emotion were not generally her thing. She pulled away and patted my arm. "You'll be fine," she said.

I swallowed my tears. She left town, and we kept working together as before, even though we were hundreds of miles apart. Often I missed her, but as she predicted, I was fine.

———————

In 1978 the five original organizations and most of the new ones joined together in a national association with a board made up of representatives from across the country. At first our new entity was called "Working Women." Later, we changed the name to "9 to 5, National Association of Working Women."

As the new national organization took shape, other 9 to 5'ers besides Karen began to move on too. Judith headed to Los Angeles to direct a chapter there. Having helped to lead our spectacularly successful campaign for better job conditions at the First National Bank, she was ready for even greater challenges. Dottie Hayden, the chair of our legal secretaries' committee in Boston, moved to Seattle, Washington, to launch a new chapter there. Anne Schick, the chair of our publishing committee, moved to Hartford, Connecticut, to start a chapter, and Diane Teichert was directing a chapter in Baltimore and would eventually found one in Atlanta.

Janet was still at her desk at the Y, still munching on carrots and celery sticks as she made her phone calls. But now, instead of talking with local office workers, she was the director of our national expansion campaign, on the phone all day with Judith, Dottie, Anne, Diane, and others across the country. She served as a vital lifeline for those starting out on the path we'd traveled just a few years before, providing these new organizers with constant contact and regular reminders that they were part of something important. She knew they needed to feel they were learning and growing, and so she supplied them with frequent evaluations of their work, along with regular doses of recognition from people both inside and outside the organization.

Janet traveled the country to make on-site visits and brought the new organizers together for regional training in the nuts and bolts of getting a group off the ground and keeping it going. She boiled down the goals of a citywide working women's organization into three key points:

New 9 to 5 chapters sprang up in Baltimore and other cities. *Schlesinger Library, Harvard Radcliffe Institute*

1. A large **base of active support** from women office workers. Continuous outreach through leafleting, surveying, lunches, events, and press.
2. **Actions targeting government officials and employers.** Demands that lead to victories that can be publicly claimed.
3. Ongoing **development** of members and leaders. Members serving as spokespeople.

Janet's training sessions offered pointers on women's legal rights, working with the media, fundraising, staff supervision, public speaking, and more. One example of the advice provided was a concise guide to engaging with government and corporate targets.

Engaging with Government and Corporate Targets

By confronting officials, we apply pressure for change. Just as important, we create a public image. The more well-organized, serious, and unified we appear, the more we will become a force to be reckoned with. A few suggestions:

1. **Before the action:** Plan. Be clear on the goal of the action. Prepare members to make statements and ask questions. Make several demands. Aim for at least one yes.

2. **At the action:** Don't wait for the "confrontee" to begin the conversation. The spokeswoman should take control by starting the meeting and reading her statement with spirit. Members should be assigned to ask questions.
   If the "confrontee" rambles and refuses to answer directly, interrupt him to bring him back to the point.
   The spokesperson should end the meeting.

3. **After the action:** Caucus. Were your demands met? Are you satisfied, disappointed, hopeful? Unless you give a clear answer, the press will make up an interpretation that may not reflect what actually happened. In meeting the press, be prepared to answer these questions:
   - Why are you here today?
   - What were your demands? Were they met?
   - How will you follow up?
   - How many members do you have? (Possible answers: the number of women active in the organization, the circulation of your newsletter, the number of phone calls you receive.)

Organizers around the country put Janet's advice to good use. Jevne Diaz remembered gathering at lunchtime with a group of brave women in the inner courtyard of a major insurance company in Atlanta. As planned, the group's chants bounced off the walls and caused a deafening din. Then they stormed the human resources office to demand job posting and career ladders.

On occasion, Janet was called on to handle meltdowns. One day a memo arrived in the mail from our Atlanta chapter. "This week has been pure hell!" a staffer had scrawled on organizational stationery. "I HATE reporters, banks, women office workers who need raises, rights, and respect. I hate TV stations! I have gone from severe burnout to *disintegration*." She was ready to quit.

Janet wrote right back with a fake news release: BREAKING NEWS! ORGANIZER RESIGNS; BANKERS BREATHE SIGH OF RELIEF.

The staffer stayed on for years and did great work.

Soon we had two dozen chapters across the country in cities large and small, including Cincinnati, Ohio; Denver, Colorado; Honolulu, Hawaii; Lincoln, Nebraska; Muncie, Indiana; Tucson, Arizona; State College, Pennsylvania; and Seattle, Washington. Later we expanded even further.

In going national, we achieved several long-standing goals. First, we received national media coverage. By the end of the 1970s, we were appearing regularly in the *New York Times*, the *Chicago Tribune*, *Newsweek*, *U.S. News & World Report*, and *People*. The news services AP and UPI covered us, and their articles were carried in newspapers large and small all over the country. The women's magazines—*Glamour*, *Redbook*, *Working Woman*—covered us too. Typical headlines:

FEMALE OFFICE HELP FED UP WITH CHORES, STAGE REBELLION
WORKING WOMEN BUCKING BOSSES
OFFICE WORKERS' REVOLT SPREADS ACROSS NATION
SECRETARIES IN REVOLT

The national media coverage in turn resulted in more new contacts than ever before. Calls poured in from women who wanted to form chapters. In 1980, after Karen and Pat, the chair of Boston 9 to 5, appeared on *The Phil Donahue Show*, a nationwide daytime talk show, we were flooded with hundreds of letters and calls. And when our organization was mentioned in the *Kiplinger Letter*, a financial journal published in Washington, DC, we received more than three thousand calls and letters. "My boss threatened to fire me if I joined," one woman wrote, "so it sounded like something I should look into."

Another benefit of going national: as we grew, we became a multiracial organization that reflected the diversity of the US office workforce—a goal we were proud to achieve. Until 1960 it was difficult for Black women to get hired as clerical workers. (In fact, in a 1940 government survey, more than 50 percent of employers stated that they had a policy against hiring Black women as clerical workers.) But beginning in 1960, the number of women of color in the office began to rise rapidly. By 1979 nearly a third of Black women nationwide were working as clericals—a figure almost as high as that for White women. The percentage of women of Puerto Rican background who were employed as clerical workers also rose, from 13 percent in 1960 to nearly one-third by the end of the 1970s.

As hiring barriers fell, pay improved significantly for office women of color. By the mid-1970s, the earnings of Black women clerical workers came close to those of White women. Latina women, too, saw their earnings increase relative to those of White women. Promotions opened up as well. During the 1970s both Black and White women moved up the ladder into professional, technical, and managerial jobs in the office at a higher rate than before. Black women didn't have as many opportunities to advance as White women did, as indicated by the fact that young Black women who were clerical workers in 1972 were more likely than White women to remain in clerical jobs by 1980. (Asian women, who earned more on average than women of other races, were less likely to be employed as clericals.)

Both in the 9 to 5 organization and later in our union, building a multiracial organization required a deliberate approach. We placed a priority on expanding into cities where the office workforce was racially diverse, such as Cleveland, Baltimore, Atlanta, and Milwaukee. We paid close attention to diversity on our board and staff. We surveyed clerical workers about patterns of race discrimination and publicized our findings. One member reported that all the Black clerical workers at her firm worked on just one floor. Women told us that the frontline, visible office jobs tended to be filled by White workers, while the less visible, lower-paying jobs went to Black women. We publicized these patterns and called on employers to end them.

Organizer Valarie Long remembered: "I was able to experience a movement of women that really tackled the race issues. We were all about being a team of women across race, but recognizing that race mattered. It wasn't uncomfortable or awkward, in my experience, and I think that's rare. It always takes work. We put women forward *and* race forward. We did a good job."

Going national enabled us to raise the money we needed to sustain our organization. Nationwide, statistics showed that only a tiny percentage of charitable money went to women's organizations. Through concerted effort, though, we were able to make successful appeals to funders in both the public and private sectors. Without these funds, we wouldn't have survived.

Going national meant we could conduct a series of nationwide campaigns. During the years when the United States had a president who was hostile to antidiscrimination measures, we defended the regulations from attack. When a more favorable administration came in, we sought to strengthen the regs. We lit a fire under the banking industry nationwide. As computers began to transform America's offices, we spoke up on behalf of office workers across the country. As we mounted pressure on employers throughout the United States, we saw improvements in city after city and in one office industry after another.

At the end of 1976, as President Gerald Ford was about to leave office, his administration announced plans to weaken the federal affirmative action program by slashing the number of companies covered by the regulations. We mobilized our multicity network—and made it personal with a flyer featuring a headshot of the official who was overseeing the cutbacks. DON'T LET THIS MAN TAKE AWAY YOUR RIGHTS, read the headline. At the bottom of the page was a tear-off section to be mailed straight to his desk in Washington, DC.

We won. The outgoing Ford administration abandoned the proposed cuts, and when President Jimmy Carter came in, we were able to not just defend but strengthen enforcement. Carter's invigorated effort found that National City Bank in Cleveland owed $15 million in back pay to women and people of color, and Third National Bank in Dayton owed $1 million. Harris Trust and Savings Bank in Chicago was found liable for $12.2. million in back pay, and Chase Manhattan Bank in New York agreed to pay $2 million.

We pressed for fair job policies at banks across the country. *Steve Cagan*

And in a small city in Kentucky in 1979, one of our members who worked at a bank overheard a young male employee boasting that his salary was higher than hers. She filed charges and won $50,000 for herself and her coworkers.

Across the country, banks began to change their ways. New training and promotion programs were launched and fat raises were awarded. In Baltimore in 1979, our chapter launched a "clean up banking" campaign, complete with a giant broom. Soon thereafter, six banks handed out more than $6 million in raises. In Providence, Rhode Island Hospital Trust National Bank awarded bonuses totaling $300,000 for two thousand low-level employees. At Cleveland's five largest banks, the proportion of women officials and managers rose by more than 20 percent in three years.

When President Ronald Reagan came into office in 1981, once again we needed to defend the antidiscrimination regulations. Picking up where Ford had left off, Reagan sought to reduce the number of companies covered by affirmative action rules, this time by 75 percent, and to eliminate back pay awards altogether. We mounted protests from coast to coast, and the administration pulled back the plan—though, alas, the $15 million back pay finding at National City Bank was rescinded.

Again making use of our national reach, we were able to make the voice of clerical workers heard from coast to coast as offices began to automate. We surveyed office workers, issued reports about our findings, and introduced protective state legislation. Desktop computers—then known as video display terminals, or VDTs—first appeared in offices at the beginning of the 1970s, and as the decade progressed, they became commonplace. At the time we had no inkling of how radically the new technology would change not only the office but also life itself across the globe. Nonetheless, we knew something big was underway.

Proponents of the new machines gushed that they would usher in a bright new world, but based on what office workers were reporting, we weren't so sure. The new technology was touted as an avenue to more fulfilling jobs, but as we made clear in our 1985 study, *Hidden Victims: Clerical Workers, Automation, and the Changing Economy*, things seemed to be heading in the opposite direction.

No one was sorry to say goodbye to correction tape and Wite-Out or the retyping of documents. We knew we couldn't stop the new technology, and we didn't want to. But many women's jobs were becoming *more* tedious, not less. The effects of the new technology were especially severe among employees working in customer service call centers, which were becoming a major way for businesses and public agencies to interact with customers and clients. Employers could have used the new technology as a tool to improve performance and customer service. Instead, for the most part they chose a more shortsighted path, and working conditions took a dive. The new technology enabled employers to monitor workers by the second and the fraction of a second. Workers were required to stick to a rigidly controlled script and meet a stringent quota. If they didn't, they risked being written up, denied a raise, or worse.

The result of these new trends was a rise in fatigue, eyestrain, backaches, and carpal tunnel syndrome—a painful condition in wrists and hands caused by repetitive motion. Stress skyrocketed. In fact, a federal study was soon to find that clericals working full-time in front of computer screens suffered the highest rate of workplace stress ever recorded— higher even than air traffic controllers. Concerns were also raised that sitting in front of a glowing screen for eight hours a day might cause miscarriages or fetal abnormalities—though in the end, no hard evidence emerged about hazards for pregnant women or their babies.

———————————

Meanwhile, back in Boston, we were preparing for our biggest event ever. To mark our fifth anniversary, we reserved the ballroom at the Sheraton Hotel for a Working Women's Convention to be held on a Saturday in November 1978. We set a goal of 750 attendees, each of whom would pay five dollars for admission. Week after week, the office bustled with activity as we made countless phone calls, shuffled endless stacks of index cards, kept a poster-sized tally of women who'd registered to come, and rehearsed our speeches again and again.

For our keynote speaker, we set our sights on Senator Ted Kennedy. We mobilized people from all across the Massachusetts power structure to call his office and urge him to come. His staff said they'd never witnessed such an intensive pressure campaign.

It worked. He said yes!

Early in the morning of the appointed day, a line of women snaked through the hotel lobby into the ballroom, which was resplendent with sparkling chandeliers, a deep-red carpet, and row upon row of upholstered folding chairs. By the time Pat opened the proceedings, a thousand women had assembled. When Senator Kennedy swept in with his entourage, the star power was thrilling. He started his remarks by thanking "my good friend Ellen Cassedy" (we'd never met), and I can't remember anything else he said.

We announced the filing of a discrimination claim against a major insurance company. Workshops on how to speak up on the job lasted into the afternoon. And when Pat read out a letter from Jane Fonda saying she was working on a new film, a comedy about office workers called *9 to 5*, the applause was deafening.

―――――――――

The next morning I woke up smiling, electrified by the scenes from the big, festive event that danced through my head. I wanted the glow to go on and on.

"Let's get married," I said to Jeff, and he said yes.

In the nearly seven years we'd been together, we'd long since chosen the menu for our wedding dinner, from the stuffed mushroom hors d'oeuvres to the carrot cake for dessert. Nonetheless, we'd hesitated to take the leap. Now we felt ready . . . sort of.

My mother came to town to help me buy a dress—a cream-colored cotton skirt and vest sprinkled with tiny brown flowers. The ceremony took place at a musty old mansion. Karen and Jeff's brother served as witnesses. Instead of vows, we recited words from a folk song that seemed to describe us to a T:

> On my way to work, I think of you . . .
> Working at the beginning of a story
> Without knowing the end

A 9 to 5'er who was enrolled in culinary school was our caterer, and the stuffed mushrooms were everything we'd imagined. Although the lemon chicken was somewhat raw, as far as I know no one got sick. My father gave a toast that cleverly intertwined the themes of organizing and starting a family, urging us to "go forth and multiply."

After dinner, our friends put on a skit. We felt giddy, buoyed up by a loving community. The evening closed with a rousing rendition of "Solidarity," the classic labor song:

> When the union's inspiration through the workers' blood
>   shall run
> There can be no power greater anywhere beneath the sun . . .
> Yet what force on earth is weaker than the feeble strength
>   of one?
> For the union makes us strong!

We loved the wedding and were surprised to find that afterward our life felt very different. It was as if the long-standing question of getting married had blocked our view of the road ahead. Now a new world of possibilities opened up. To my surprise, I realized I didn't want to live in our apartment anymore. I didn't want to work at the Y anymore. I didn't want to live in Boston anymore. Like other 9 to 5'ers, I was hungry for new challenges and ready to move on.

I talked it over with Karen and Janet, and a plan took shape. Beginning in the fall of 1979, I would become the director of the office we'd opened in Washington, DC, and represent our organization at meetings of the women's and civil rights groups that were working to keep the federal enforcement effort on track. Jeff was up for a move too. Like ours, his community organization was going national, and someone was needed to start a new branch in Pennsylvania. The two of us took a long walk, had a long talk, and decided to move to Philadelphia. Jeff would start his new statewide consumer organization, and I would spend half of each week in Philadelphia and the other half in Washington, with a desk in both cities.

Making a plan for a new life together was exhilarating. We went down to Philadelphia to explore. Unlike Boston, the city was sprawling and spacious. The crowd on the downtown sidewalks was more racially diverse than in Boston, and so was the city leadership. The industrial sector was visible everywhere: a giant oil refinery and vast scrap-metal yards assaulted your senses as you entered town, and the factory buildings went on for miles—though many of them were abandoned, with shuttered or shattered windows. The huge neon sign atop the public employees' union building near the train station trumpeted the presence of the local labor movement. It was a big and exciting new arena.

My replacement as director in Boston was Joan Quinlan, a member of our staff who was eager for the challenge. She moved right into my cubicle. The transition was seamless.

During my last days in Boston, in the fall of 1979, I would look around my tiny space, taking in the desk with one drawer pull missing, the stack of file folders that had been labeled over and over, the bulletin board pocked with thumbtack holes, the dusty window overlooking the John Hancock Tower. I couldn't wait to leave.

I counted the minutes through the goodbye scenes. Goodbye to Ken's at Copley and the no. 1 breakfast with its scrap of scrambled egg. Goodbye to the golden State House dome and the Public Garden I'd hurried across on the way to so many lunch meetings. Goodbye to the map of downtown imprinted on my brain, which showed exactly where to stand to distribute the most leaflets in the least time. Goodbye to all the ZIP codes I'd memorized during our newsletter mailing parties and the Boston-area telephone exchanges I knew by heart. Goodbye to City Hall Plaza, the site of our National Secretaries Day rallies, to the squealing Green Line trolleys and the rest of the T system I knew so well, and to the narrow streets of Somerville, my hometown, with its three-deckers and handkerchief yards.

And goodbye to the 9 to 5 members with whom I'd designed strategies and crafted agendas and practiced speeches and celebrated so many victories.

It was a lot to leave behind, but somehow I didn't feel sad. Instead, I felt proud to be leaving a vibrant organization in place as I moved on to somewhere new. I had no doubt that Boston 9 to 5 would flourish in my absence. Besides, I reminded myself, I wasn't really leaving. I was just relocating to another part of our movement.

Jeff left for Philadelphia a month before I did. He had to get his new organization off the ground right away, he said, which meant that unfortunately he wouldn't be able to help with the packing. My mother came up to Boston to help me dismantle the kitchen and wrap up all our wedding presents (minus a set of cordial glasses from Uncle David that I couldn't imagine ever using). When we opened Jeff's dresser and discovered that he owned nearly two dozen identical blue sweaters, we collapsed on the bed in giggles and couldn't stop laughing. Maybe I was more nervous about leaving town than I realized.

The day the movers came, I begged a friend to come over and keep me company. He started a fire in the toaster oven that was still ablaze when the men came up the stairs. Otherwise, all went well. Jeff drove up from Philadelphia the next day. We loaded the car with the last hard-to-pack items and set off down the highway.

We rented an apartment in a charming brick building covered with ivy (in fact, as we discovered the hard way, it was poison ivy), and two different nonprofit organizations gave us space for our respective desks. On weekends, we toured the Liberty Bell and Independence Hall, the science museum with its walk-in human heart, and Fairmount Park with its vast lawns. On New Year's Day, we were invited to a party in an apartment high above Broad Street, where we stood at the window blinking in disbelief at the Mummers Parade, a bizarre annual phenomenon featuring men prancing down the street in giant feather boas.

Every Tuesday afternoon, I'd get on the train for the three-hour ride to Washington, DC. I'd arrive at Union Station as the pink rays of sunset were tinting the monuments and the government buildings. For two or three days, I'd traipse in and out of congressional buildings and agency offices along with representatives of a dozen antidiscrimination groups— the Leadership Conference on Civil Rights, the NAACP Legal Defense Fund, the National Organization for Women, the League of United Latin American Citizens, and more. I ran press conferences and testified at hearings. The spirited demonstrations that 9 to 5 was mounting and the press coverage we were receiving across the country gave my words extra punch when I spoke.

At the end of each day, I'd head for my desk inside the office of a DC think tank to listen to my voice-mail messages and draft testimony. I spent nights in a basement room I'd rented from a friend, warming up my dinner in a toaster oven and sleeping on a mattress on the floor. It was a far cry from the homey office at the Boston Y, with its unending chatter, its screams of joy, and its sympathetic shoulders to cry on when things didn't go well.

I represented 9 to 5 in Washington, DC, as we targeted the banking industry. *Author's collection (top), Schlesinger Library, Harvard Radcliffe Institute (bottom)*

On Thursday or Friday, I'd get back on the train and return to Philadelphia. Jeff was often out of town, drumming up support for his new organization in faraway Pittsburgh or Erie or Harrisburg. I spent my evenings at home in the new apartment with the same book or magazine that had kept me company on the train. I was lonely.

Now that I was no longer in daily contact with my longtime bosom buddies, I looked forward eagerly to our Summer School for Working Women. Starting in July 1979, the annual gathering was an opportunity to renew ties and store up inspiration for the year to come. Hundreds of women came together from New York, San Francisco, Cleveland, Chicago, Baltimore, Los Angeles, Milwaukee, Atlanta, Pittsburgh, Dayton, and more. One year, Ellen Bravo got in a car and drove eighteen hours to attend. On her name tag, she wrote SOON-TO-BE MILWAUKEE CHAPTER, and when she got back home, the new chapter took off.

For several years we met at Bryn Mawr, a women's college on the leafy outskirts of Philadelphia. More than fifty years earlier, the college had been home to a similar gathering, the Bryn Mawr Summer School for Women Workers in Industry, founded in 1921 to promote "equal opportunity for the manual workers of the world . . . by utilizing the deep sex sympathy that women now feel for each other." Now the torch was being passed.

We sat together on the green lawns and walked the paths lined with plane trees. The venerable old meeting halls with their lead-paned windows and vaulted ceilings were alive with colorful banners. We could sense our activist foremothers whispering in our ears and urging us forward as

Women came to the 9 to 5 summer school from all over the country. *Steve Cagan*

we immersed ourselves in historical and economic education and intensive training in organizing skills. Every night there were skits and guest speakers. There was a special gathering of "lesbians and their friends." One year a singer entertained us with a lament in the voice of the nation's bosses:

> Whatever will we do, whatever on this earth,
> When all the secretaries demand what they are worth?

All of us were thrilled when Jane Fonda came to the very first summer school to gather material for her film *9 to 5*. Dressed in the same pink T-shirt we were all wearing, with its slogan RAISES, NOT ROSES, she sat on the grass and listened as women shared their stories and their dreams.

The film would turn out to be a big hit—and a huge boost for our movement.

13

HOLLYWOOD

KAREN HAD MET JANE FONDA in the peace movement, and after the Vietnam War ended in 1975, they stayed in touch. Jane (as we all came to refer to her) was famous both for her acting and for her activism. When she told Karen that she wanted to help our cause by making a movie about office workers, we were thrilled.

Jane was the daughter of Henry Fonda, an actor best known for his role in *The Grapes of Wrath* (1940), based on John Steinbeck's novel about an Oklahoma family that migrates to California during the Great Depression. Beginning in the 1960s, she began building a robust acting career of her own. She played a daring outlaw in *Cat Ballou* (1965) and a steamy sex symbol in *Barbarella* (1968), a science fiction spoof that became a cult classic. She won awards for her portrayal of a call girl in *Klute* (1971); her shag hairstyle in that movie became so popular that even my great-aunt Jessie, who lived in a nursing home, started wearing it.

When the Vietnam War heated up, so did Jane's activism. As part of a group of actors, she toured military towns and college campuses with a show called *Free the Army*, and in 1972 she visited Hanoi. The FBI and CIA began tapping her phone and monitoring her mail, and she became a controversial figure.

Controversy or no, Jane was lauded as one of the finest actors of her time. She won Academy Awards and many other prizes. She had an extraordinary range, shining in comic roles as well as serious ones. In 1976

153

she and a business partner founded IPC Films, a production company focused on social issues.

Karen had kept Jane well informed about 9 to 5. Jane knew all about the bank tellers who were paid so little that they were living on food stamps, and about the woman who was fired for bringing her boss a corned beef sandwich on white bread instead of rye.

Now, as she prepared to make her movie about office workers, she wanted to learn more. One of her writers, Patricia Resnick, had been an office worker; she'd even gotten a job at a large insurance company to collect material for the script. But writer-director Colin Higgins (best known for the 1971 film *Harold and Maude*) knew little about the subject.

In 1978 when Jane asked if she could bring her team to meet some of our members, we gathered a group of thirty or forty women after work in our Cleveland office. After introductions, Higgins posed a question that somehow we'd never thought to ask in all our years of recruitment lunches: "Have you ever fantasized about killing your boss?"

At first there was silence. Then nervous giggles. Finally, one woman raised her hand. She often imagined pulverizing her boss in a coffee grinder, she said, allowing the grounds to drip into the carafe, and then, well, drinking him.

The room exploded. One after another, women chimed in with their dreams of revenge. There was an electrocution fantasy. A cyanide fantasy. A fantasy about spinning a boss around in his swivel chair and launching him out the window. Jane's team ate it up, and the gruesome scenarios went into the mix, along with true tales of workplace indignities and hard facts about pay and promotions.

The studio moguls were skeptical. Was there really an audience for what Jane was proposing? Even though one out of three working women was an office worker, you couldn't find a film with an office worker as the central character. In the 1930s there was Della Street, who was both the secretary and the love interest of detective Perry Mason. In the 1950s Ann Sothern played "Susie the Secretary" in a TV drama about a talent agency. But that was about it. Although there were millions of us, we were pretty much invisible. Karen wrote a background memo for Jane to take to the studio. "Talk to these women," she wrote, "and they will talk back."

Jane's first inclination was to make a serious movie. But as she remembered it, one day on the radio she heard Dolly Parton singing her song "Two Doors Down," about a woman who pulls herself out of a funk and goes after what she wants. Listening to the song, she had a vision of Dolly, with her long painted fingernails, working as a secretary. She'd long wanted to work with Lily Tomlin, and she decided to ask both of them to join the cast.

"Write a screenplay," she instructed Higgins, "which shows you can run an office without the boss, but you can't run an office without the secretaries."

The result was the blockbuster 1980 comedy *9 to 5*, starring the three women, with Dabney Coleman as the evil boss. Why a comedy? "The stories we heard from secretaries," Jane's partner Bruce Gilbert explained to the *Washington Post*, "were often so outrageous that no one would believe them if they were played as straight drama."

Jane was determined that the film not be preachy. "I'm just supersensitive to anything that smacks of the soapbox or lecturing the audience," she told the *Times* of London. Again and again, as the production proceeded, she insisted that lines and scenes be cut because they were too didactic.

Unlike Jane, we did want to preach. We liked to laugh and poke fun, but we also had a very earnest streak. For us, some jokes were not one bit funny. Around the time that Jane's film was in development, for example, a TV game show began airing nationwide with the tagline "Who knows a man better, his wife or his secretary?" Three-person teams (boss, wife, and secretary) competed against one another, and prizes were awarded for correct answers to questions like these: "Bosses! What is the sexiest thing your secretary ever wore just for you?" "Secretaries! What's the sign of affection your boss is most known for?" "Wives! Is your husband's secretary too sexy or not sexy enough?" We were not amused. Our chapter in Los Angeles circulated a petition demanding that the show be pulled, and after less than five months on the air, it was.

What if the film got it all wrong? We asked if we could put someone on the set to keep an eye on things, and Jane's production team agreed.

Janice, a member of our national staff who was based in Boston, moved to Los Angeles for several months, and Jane and her then-husband, Tom Hayden, generously invited her into their house as their guest.

Janice spent every day on the set watching to make sure there were no wrong notes. An early version, for example, had the office worker characters ordering avocado sandwiches for lunch, a detail that might have rung true in California but not elsewhere in the United States in the early 1980s. Janice spoke up doggedly on behalf of our key principles: The film would have to show respect for office workers. It would have to make clear that it was the unfair boss who was the problem, not the women themselves. The focus had to be on women's work lives, not their personal lives, and on how clerical jobs could be made better, not on how women could get out of those jobs. The film would have to portray not just the problems but the solutions—our Bill of Rights and more. And the means to those solutions had to be women banding together.

We were dismayed when we learned that as the plot proceeded, the action moved out of the office into a bar, then a hospital, then the boss's McMansion. Janice kept on weighing in, but her influence was limited. We became increasingly anxious.

One thing we didn't have to worry about was the actors. They were a dream. Jane had long since proved herself on-screen, and the other members of the trio, though new to moviemaking, had enormous charisma.

Lily Tomlin was a great comic force, best known for the character of Ernestine, a take-no-prisoners switchboard operator whose signature line was "Is this the party to whom I am speaking?" She was drawn to 9 to 5 in part because of her experiences as a waitress and office temp in years past. "You'd go a little berserk being a waitress," she said. "Then you'd go back to being an office temp, then you'd go berserk, then you'd go back to being a waitress."

Dolly Parton was a superstar as a singer, songwriter, and record producer who regularly hit the top of the charts in both country and pop music. She styled herself as an outrageous caricature, recognizable far and wide by her huge blond wig, surgically enhanced bosom, and skintight clothing. About her many plastic surgeries, she was unapologetic. "It takes a lot of money to look this cheap," she often joked. Born in a one-room cabin in Tennessee into a family with twelve children, she treasured her connection with her country roots and knew that working with Jane might be a risk to her career. Audiences sometimes booed when she mentioned Jane, but Dolly was a confirmed bridge builder who threaded a careful political line. She nurtured a huge fan base that spanned south and north, conservative and progressive, gay and straight.

One day she arrived on the *9 to 5* set and took out her guitar. "I've got a song," she announced. Simulating the sound of typing, she clicked her fingernails to establish the beat. Then she launched into what became one of her biggest hits.

Her song "9 to 5" perfectly encapsulates our movement. It starts with an awakening and with pride, moves on to grievances, and directs some angry energy at management. Then it summons a sense of collective power:

> In the same boat with a lot of your friends
> Waitin' for the day your ship'll come in

And finally it ends in triumph:

> And the tide's gonna turn an' it's all gonna roll your way

The song reached the top of the charts. With its combination of what one writer called "angry complaint and immense good cheer," it remained a popular favorite for decades.

The actors had a ball with *9 to 5*. While director Higgins had "expected some tension" in working with the three stars, he found them "totally professional, great fun and a joy to work with." The production process was sisterly. "I just wish everything would be as easy," Higgins said. Jane was cool and businesslike on the set, Lily ad-libbed and improvised her way through the shoot, and Dolly, who had never before appeared in a movie, was a quick study. "There's no sense of competition," Dolly told *Newsweek*. "It's just a real love project."

The roles were tailor-made for the three women. Jane played Judy Bernly, naive, primly attired, and new to the workforce after her husband runs off with his secretary. Lily was Violet Newstead, the ultracompetent, ultraconfident office veteran who's been passed over for

promotion in favor of a young man she trained. Dolly was Doralee
Rhodes, a sweet young woman mightily annoyed by her boss's lecher-
ous attentions.

If it was our movement that had given rise to the movie, now Jane
worked closely with us to make sure that the movie would build the movement. At the end of September 1979, a little more than a year before the
film was released, she and Tom Hayden conducted a thirty-day, fifty-city
tour to promote their California organization, the Campaign for Economic
Democracy. In Boston Jane hosted a brown-bag lunch in honor of "the
economic rights of working women" at a donated movie theater. The
event lasted just forty minutes, from 12:10 to 12:50 PM, so that women
could attend on their lunch hour. Tickets were five dollars apiece (four
dollars for 9 to 5 members).

This time we didn't need to activate our phone trees. The women
just came—more than a thousand of them. A yogurt company begged us
to pass out free containers of a new drink to everyone who came in the
door, and we agreed. Speaking from a podium onstage, our chairwoman,
Pat, praised yogurt as "the staple of the working women's diet," then
introduced Jane as "an intelligent person, a respected individual, and a
working woman from California."

To thunderous applause, Jane came out wearing her pink RAISES,
NOT ROSES T-shirt. "Some people want to know why I'm interested in
women office workers," she said. "I was one, and I was fired because I
wouldn't sleep with my boss. I also found the work too hard, so I went
into acting."

The audience roared and clapped, and kept on clapping when she
urged women to fight for justice on the job and settle for nothing less
than our Bill of Rights.

When the power suddenly failed—the lights went off and the mic
stopped working—Jane kept on talking. "Comedy is the flip side of trag-
edy," she said. "If I had to sum up the film in one sentence, it's about
women office workers who fantasize about murdering their boss." Laughter and cheers. "The women kidnap their boss, and no one ever finds out
he's not there."

Across the country, Jane served as an articulate spokeswoman for our
cause. "No business can run without office workers," she told the media.

"It's skilled work. These women work hard, and they deserve justice." When the *Cleveland Press* asked her if she was trying to light a fire under office desks, she responded, "No, secretaries across the country have lit the fires. We're just fanning the flames."

Before and after the movie came out, Jane held outdoor rallies for working women in city after city. For National Secretaries Week in 1979 in San Francisco, seven thousand people heard her speak outdoors at Embarcadero Plaza. The next year, on the last day of shooting the film, she came straight from the set to a downtown Los Angeles hotel, still wearing her wig (and the pink T-shirt), and won a standing ovation from an overflow crowd of two thousand office workers. She appeared in a photo in *U.S. News & World Report* in 1979 handing out leaflets for our organization and was the subject of a *New York Times* article the same year with the headline JANE FONDA TO OFFICE WORKERS: "ORGANIZE." All of this gave our organization new visibility and validation on a giant scale.

The movie was released right before Christmas in 1980. All over the country, our members held celebratory "office parties of the year." I went to New York for the premiere. As I approached the Sutton Theatre in Midtown Manhattan, my heart started pounding. A huge searchlight was parked on the sidewalk, projecting a rotating beam high into the sky. A poster depicted Dabney Coleman tied up in his office chair, surrounded by Jane chatting merrily on the phone, Lily winking at the camera as she poured him a cup of coffee, and Dolly pertly brandishing a steno pad. Crowds of special guests streamed in. Some were Hollywood types in formal attire. Others, also dressed to the nines, were office women who'd won the lucky tickets in the raffle we ran.

As the movie begins, the sound of typewriter keys fills your ears over the thumping beat of Dolly's song. To me, those opening bars evoked our first 9 to 5 newsletter, with its fresh, welcoming headline: EVERY MORNING . . . We see office towers soaring into the sky and hundreds of legs hurrying to work through streets and plazas, one woman hailing a taxi, another checking her watch with a coffee cup balanced in one hand and a purse in the other. Dressed in a baby-blue suit and a matching hat, Jane as Judy Bernly squeezes into a packed elevator and reports for her first

Our organizing inspired the 1980 Hollywood
film. *Author's collection—movie poster*

day of work at Consolidated Companies, a megafirm whose business is
never specified. We see employees punching the time clock and feel the
buzz as we enter the bustling hive of Consolidated. The details of office
life fill the screen—a sea of desks, dozens of desktop phones with multiple
blinking buttons, staplers and paper clips and swivel chairs, typewriters
and coffee mugs. Violet shows Judy the ropes, introducing her to Doralee
and to the boss, Mr. Hart, whom a *New York Times* reviewer characterized
as "a fine, lunatic villain, a mini-brained tomcat."

Tensions rise. One after another, the three women reach a boiling
point. "Something," Violet predicts, "is going to snap." Sure enough, the
three office mates soon storm out of the office and decamp to a nearby
bar. There they sit, sharing their stories and trying to figure out what to
do. By the time they move on to Dolly's house for dinner, they've become
a team. (When we saw Violet take out a joint in that scene to share along
with the barbecued ribs, we were horrified. Now, of course, I realize that
our precious members were likely not nearly as scandalized as we feared.)

Helped along by the marijuana, the women let their imaginations run wild, and here's where our members' vengeful fantasies came in. A torch-wielding mob of employees chases the terrified Hart through the corridors of Consolidated. He takes shelter in a corner and thinks he's safe, but no—Judy pops up from behind a desk in a safari outfit. Raising a hunting rifle, she fixes him in her sights and calls him out as a "sexist, egotistical, lying, hypocritical bigot." Doralee torments Hart with the same kind of humiliating harassment he's been subjecting her to, ordering him to take dictation while she ogles his crotch—before roping him with a lasso and roasting him on a spit. Then comes Violet, dressed in a Disneyesque dirndl, smiling sweetly as she offers a cup of poisoned coffee.

Echoes of these violent fantasies reemerge later as it becomes necessary for the women to imprison Hart in chains in his own luxurious home. There are scenes with a dead body in the trunk of a car, a scurry through the halls of a hospital, the discovery of an embezzlement scheme, and on and on.

Meanwhile, back at the office, with the boss out of the way, the three women take over. No one except Roz, the officious supervisor, is the slightest bit sorry that he's missing. A series of orders goes out bearing his forged signature. His ban on photos and plants on the desktops is rescinded. A job-sharing policy is put in place, an addiction recovery program launched. Job openings are posted on the bulletin board. An empty storage room becomes a bustling childcare center. In a matter of weeks, the women have implemented our Bill of Rights.

Just as we had hoped, the women characters are utterly central. In fact, aside from the boss, men have very few lines. You hardly ever see more than one of them in a room at once. What would happen if you took the boss out of the office? What would happen if women got together? The answer was as plain as day.

Reviews were mixed. "Pleasant," said one critic. "A lot of fun," said another.

"A leering, doddering movie," said a third. "Slick." "Preposterous." "Borders on the inane."

"Overly complicated." "Coarse." "Male pigs, unevenly roasted."

But if the critics were lukewarm, audience reaction was through the roof. The mood in the theaters was electric. Millions of working women were starved for a reflection of themselves in the mass media. Now, seeing themselves on-screen, they gasped, hooted, applauded, and shouted out advice. There were shrieks of laughter, waves of applause, shouts of "Right on!"

In one early scene, Judy is ushered into the copy room and left alone with a giant machine. Like the broom in the "Sorcerer's Apprentice" segment of the Disney film *Fantasia*, the copier has a mind of its own. Faster and faster, sheets of paper begin emerging from various orifices, slotting themselves into multiple trays, and flying onto the floor as Judy scrambles to collect them. Her lip begins to tremble. At this point, women in the audience would stand up and yell, "Push the stop button!"

The film had a more universal appeal than anyone had anticipated. Even men liked it. Some of them had fantasized about doing in their bosses too.

9 to 5 was the second-highest-grossing film of 1980, after *The Empire Strikes Back*, another epic battle between good and evil. It became the twentieth-highest-grossing comedy of all time.

We didn't share in any of the money. But what we did get was priceless. To the ideas of the women's movement and the power of the labor movement, we added the glamour of Hollywood. It all worked together. Our impact grew bigger than ever before.

––––––––

After the premiere, Karen traveled to twenty cities to promote the "movement behind the movie." She'd appear on a morning TV show, between a piece on how to bake macaroni and a special on the zoo, then sit for interviews with a newspaper and a radio show. At lunchtime she'd meet with women who were interested in organizing, and in the evening a couple of hundred women would show up for a public meeting or a rally. We formed a dozen new chapters.

There were other spin-offs too. Karen and I wrote *9 to 5: The Working Woman's Guide to Office Survival*, and our publisher sent us on a fifteen-city media tour. Wearing a blue silk dress I'd bought for the occasion (a truly appropriate outfit, for once), I covered the East Coast, Houston, and Dallas, while Karen covered the Midwest and the West Coast.

A TV sitcom was created based on the movie, and once again we were allowed to place one of our staff on the set as a consultant. In 1982 it was one of the highest-ranking new TV shows. It ran for several years. In 2009 a musical version of the film opened on Broadway with new songs by Dolly Parton. It was nominated for four Tony Awards and toured the United States. Starting in 2012, a version began touring in Britain, to wild acclaim.

The most important effect of the movie was a change in public consciousness. Before the film came out, we had to argue—with women, with bosses, with policy makers, with the public—about whether there was discrimination at the workplace. We had to present proof. We had to push women to understand that they were being treated unfairly. We had to convince bosses that inequality wasn't the natural order and that women didn't actually want to be stuck in low-paying, dead-end jobs. Now the argument was over. Yes, the movie was silly. But the silliness worked. By making millions of people laugh at bosses' bad behavior, the film ended the debate. Now the question was what should be done about the situation.

And what *should* be done? In the scene at the bar, as the three stars are moaning about their problems over their drinks, Judy bursts out, "We've got to do something! Can't we—*complain*?" It's a laugh line, but as with so many lines in the film, it's a line with a serious import. For millions of women, getting past complaining was the critical challenge. Through our movement, women were joining together for change, and now the movie showed Jane, Lily, and Dolly doing the same thing. It was a vital contribution to our cause.

In an interview with the *Washington Post* when the film was released, Jane's partner Bruce Gilbert made a prediction: "Getting coffee," he said, "will never be the same after this movie comes out."

He was right.

One morning on my way to work soon after the movie opened in the theaters, I overheard two women talking on the bus. "So I said to him," one was saying, "'No, I will not! I just saw *9 to 5*, and I will *not* make your coffee. I'm never going to make another cup of coffee again!'"

For me, the best moment in our adventure with the movie took place on opening night, when Karen and I were seated near the front of the theater surrounded by the murmurs of an excited crowd. The lights went down, the rat-a-tat of Dolly's infectious song began, and the screen filled with legions of women on their way to work. Karen reached over and clasped my hand as the words rang out: "Working 9 to 5—what a way to make a living!"

14

OUR UNION
GOES NATIONAL

WITH THE MOVIE BOOSTING our visibility across the country, we sailed into the 1980s full of hope.

9 to 5 had members in forty-five states, offices in fourteen major cities, and fifty paid organizers. In dozens of cities, we had leaders who could recruit coworkers and take on the boss. Local 925, our union in Boston, had a thousand members. We had a research and program hub in Cleveland headed by Karen, an expansion and training program headed by Janet in Boston, and a Washington, DC, advocacy effort led by me. Our campaigns were covered regularly by the national media. Hundreds of thousands of women had heard of us, agreed with us, felt empowered by us.

In her keynote speech at our summer school, Karen urged us forward. This was the decade, she said, when clerical organizing was destined to grow to massive proportions, and as it did, the labor movement all across the United States would be revitalized. "Opportunities to fight always exist," she declared, "but opportunities to win come once in a lifetime. So get out your eight-by-ten glossies for the archives. There is a page for each of us, and many battles to be won." Her final words from the podium left us all in tears:

I sometimes think of myself decades from now, looking back on these days. I believe I will look back at a triumph.

We have history on our side. But *we* have to do it. We will need patience, anger, commitment, hard work, impatience, and love.

There's an old saying: "Bloom where you are planted." I think it's lovely, and it's about us. Most of us won't be becoming lawyers or housewives, or Princess Di. We're here. We're planted right here.

So, sisters, dig those roots and spread those blossoms. And let's change the world.

To dig those roots and change the world, we got ready to take our union national.

––––––––––––

At the beginning of the 1970s, George Meany, the president of the AFL-CIO, had eloquently stated his lack of interest in new union members. Yet that decade saw a big increase in union drives. And in the words of historian Lane Windham, "Women powered the new wave of unionization attempts."

To many people's surprise, women turned out to be more prounion than men. An AFL-CIO survey a few years later found that at workplaces where a majority of workers were men, most union drives failed, but where women were at least three-quarters of the workforce, most drives succeeded. The win rate was even higher where the workers were women of color. Across the country, Black workers had the highest unionization rates of any racial or ethnic group in the 1970s. By the end of the 1970s, Black women were joining unions at twice the rate of White women, and Black workers continued to have the highest unionization rate of any racial or ethnic group into the twenty-first century.

By the 1980s, a number of unions had stepped up organizing among clerical workers. The American Federation of State, County, and Municipal Employees (AFSCME) organized tens of thousands of state clerical workers in Illinois, Florida, Ohio, Pennsylvania, Iowa, and elsewhere. Mostly, but not exclusively, they approached clerical organizing within larger public employee campaigns.

"Women powered the new wave of unionization attempts." *Richard Bermack*

AFSCME won important victories on the issue of pay equity, or equal pay for work of equal value. In 1981 the city of San Jose, California, commissioned a study and found that jobs dominated by women were paid 2 percent to 10 percent below average. For example, a senior stenography clerk and a senior water system technician were rated the same, but the clerk job (female) was paid $638 per month and the technician job (male) $835. When the city refused to change the pay scales to reflect the true value of the women's jobs, fifteen hundred employees—librarians, mechanics, janitors, and clericals alike—held a ten-day strike and won pay increases totaling $1.5 million. In Washington State, AFSCME filed a pay equity lawsuit that was settled in 1985 to the tune of $482 million in back pay. And in 1989 AFSCME was the union that won the groundbreaking victory among clerical and technical employees at Harvard University.

The Communications Workers of America (CWA) represented tens of thousands of clerical workers in the telephone system, which had undergone sweeping changes. The industry was deregulated. New office technology was introduced. Call centers were moved offshore to countries with lower wages. And cell phones changed the world. CWA developed creative bargaining and organizing strategies to protect clerical workers who were already in the union and to bring in new members. Clerical workers were also part of CWA's organizing drives in industries outside the telephone system.

Through the efforts of the American Federation of Teachers (AFT) and the National Education Association (NEA), the 1960s and 1970s were years of militant organizing and bargaining among teachers. The organizing continued into the 1980s, and school secretaries were part of the action, some in local units of their own, others in locals that included other kinds of school workers.

Although the Teamsters Union is best known for representing freight drivers and warehouse workers, it also represents other kinds of employees. According to Vicki Saporta, who became the Teamsters' organizing director in 1983, "Sometimes workers are so fed up with bad bosses that they decide they need what they perceive as 'the toughest and the baddest,' so they call in the Teamsters." In 1976 the union organized two thousand clerical workers at the Blue Cross Blue Shield insurance company in Chicago, then went on to organize the clerical workers at the University of Chicago. Other Teamster wins in higher education followed in later years.

As we searched for the best place to dig our roots, spread our blossoms, and change the world at the beginning of the 1980s, we talked with representatives of several of these unions. Soon enough, however, we zeroed in once again on SEIU, the union that had chartered Local 925 in Boston in 1975. Karen took the lead in bargaining for a national charter, making the pitch that together, SEIU and 9 to 5 could lead the way in bringing a new, dynamic population into the labor movement—a population that *had* to be reached if the labor movement was to survive and grow. Although service and clerical workers were half the workforce, they were less than 20 percent of union membership. America's office workers were ready, we said, not only to join a wave of organizing but to lead that wave.

No, office workers didn't yet know much about unions, and yes, employers, who *did* know about unions, were firmly against them. (Just how firmly, we didn't yet know. We were about to find out.) But those obstacles could be overcome. They had to be overcome. And we were the ones to overcome them.

SEIU's new president, John J. Sweeney, took a chance on us, agreeing to work with us in launching a bold experiment. The agreement we made was groundbreaking. A woman-led union was unique, our focus on office workers was unique, and our nationwide charter was unique. We had our own treasury and bylaws. We elected our own officers. As with our Local 925 in Boston, we asked for and received the right to hire our own organizers and the money to pay them at the same rate as men in the union. We received enough funds to pay for Jackie Ruff and an assistant in Washington, DC, plus three organizers—Cheryl Schaffer on the East Coast, Anne Hill in the Midwest, and Bonnie Ladin on the West Coast.

Sweeney boosted SEIU's organizing budget nationwide and recognized the need to reach out to unorganized workers throughout the changing economy. He and his leadership team saw tremendous potential in the office workforce and viewed collaborating with us as a way for SEIU to set the standard for what a modern, dynamic union should do.

When Sweeney became president of the AFL-CIO a decade and a half later, in 1995, once again he increased the organizing budget. "It is a monumental task to organize any group of workers," he said, "and in an industry that is highly unorganized it takes years and years to achieve the kind of success you would like to achieve. But you cannot give up." Sweeney remained at the helm of the AFL-CIO until 2009, when he was succeeded by Rich Trumka. When Sweeney died in 2021, he was remembered for his dedication to the least powerful members of the workforce. He was also remembered for offering to bring the coffee to meetings in his office.

We launched our new union on March 3, 1981, with a splash. The name was District 925—"district" in this case indicating that the new entity was not limited to one locality but instead spread out over a large geographic area—in fact, from coast to coast. We held rallies and press conferences across the country. Articles appeared in newspapers and on TV and radio shows. Karen was announced as the acting president of the new District 925, at the same time continuing as the national director of our nonunion wing. Our special focus would be private-sector workers, we declared, especially those in the heart of the financial industry. The new District 925, we felt confident, would soon become one of SEIU's biggest units.

SEIU established a new Clerical Division. In the spring of 1981, in Storrs, Connecticut, we were prominently featured at the union's first women's conference. Locals were provided with posters and a list of suggested activities for National Secretaries Week. The union promoted bargaining points on paid sick leave, family and medical leave, equal pay, pay equity, and an end to race and sex discrimination.

We set up a nationwide toll-free hotline for office workers—a big deal in the era before cell phones and the Internet. On the launch day, Dabney Coleman, the actor who played the boss in the *9 to 5* movie, answered the phone alongside SEIU's switchboard operator. We offered a free brochure, *The 9 to 5 Survival Guide*, and eighty thousand office workers called to ask for a copy. "You are not alone," the booklet began. "There are things you can do to help yourself and ways you can join with others in winning raises, rights, and respect." We urged women to take risks, to start support groups, and to understand their legal rights, including the right to organize.

The media coverage, the hotline, the free brochures—all of it had an impact. Women began to call us asking how to join the union. Our organizers were soon running up and down the coasts and all over the Midwest, pursuing leads, making calls, scheduling meetings. They slept—when they slept—on couches at the homes of supporters and at low-budget motels.

What were we thinking? True, all three of our organizers were extraordinary women—brash powerhouses with tons of stamina. But still, one organizer for the East Coast, one for the Midwest, and one for the West Coast? Today, the whole project looks somewhat delusional.

But often in history, isn't it the people who don't know what won't work and therefore aren't afraid to try who manage to move things forward? We had no preset notions of what could and couldn't be done. With support from our parent union, we were free to follow our noses—and we did.

We got off to a strong start. Soon we had a dozen drives in progress, from Boston to Seattle. Drawing on the tactics we'd developed in the 9 to 5 organization, plus the guidance of our SEIU colleagues, we rolled out our own signature style of union organizing. Like union organizers anywhere, we did what we thought would work. But a union that was led by women and represented women was something new, and it had its own special character.

We held meetings at lunchtime instead of at night, and we provided childcare. These things seemed natural to us. We did them because we had to. But they were departures from the way most unions operated. Because we were building from scratch, we had to do things that established unions didn't necessarily do. We devoted special attention to developing leaders and building relationships with women one by one—because we had to. We drew on support from the community—because we had to. We made use of humor and surprise—because we had to. And out of necessity, we were powered by a passionate sense of solidarity and commitment. Without every one of these elements, our union wouldn't have survived.

It didn't take long for the obstacles facing us to come into focus. It became clear that all of us—District 925, SEIU as a whole, and other unions too—were swimming upstream. We'd started our national union at a time when the labor movement was being battered by powerful economic forces and fierce employer resistance. Although organizing was on the rise in the public sector, it was not enough to make up for the steep decline in the private sector.

Let's step back and take a look at what we were up against.

Coming out of World War II, the United States occupied a dominant position in the world economy. Business was booming, and many American families were sharing in the wealth. Wages rose steadily every year, and benefits kept pace. More than three-quarters of manufacturing firms in the middle of the twentieth century were covered by collective bargaining agreements, and these unionized workplaces set the standard for workplaces that didn't have unions. Between the unionized companies and the nonunionized companies that matched union wages and benefits, millions of working families reaped the rewards of cooperation between labor and management.

But by the mid-1960s, global competition began to cut into the profits of US companies. A few years later, by the 1970s, the United States was grappling with an energy crisis and a recession brought on by the Vietnam War. Inflation and unemployment rose and rose again. In the face of these problems, rather than share the pain, US corporations sought to keep profits high while shifting the burden to others. As early as 1974, a *BusinessWeek* editorial baldly spelled out what was to come:

> It is inevitable that the US economy will grow more slowly than it has. Cities and states, the home mortgage market, small business and the consumer, will all get less than they want. It will be a hard pill for many Americans to swallow—the idea of doing with less so that big business can have more. . . . Nothing that this nation or any nation has done in modern history compares in difficulty with the selling job that must now be done to make people accept the new reality.

By the 1980s, when we started District 925, the "new reality" referred to in the *BusinessWeek* editorial was in full flower. The era of labor-management cooperation that had prevailed since World War II had come to an end.

While between 1949 and 1979 blue-collar wages rose by 75 percent, now, in the 1980s, things were different. As managers' salaries skyrocketed, workers' pay slipped. Between 1979 and 2005, blue-collar wages would rise by only 2 percent (adjusted for inflation), and benefits would be slashed. In other industrial nations, workers' health care and retirement security were the responsibility of government. But in the United States, these aspects of social welfare were largely the responsibility of employers, generally in negotiation with unions. Now employers set about cutting back on these benefits. In the industrial sector, factories closed down by the thousands. Employers replaced workers with machines. They invested overseas and moved out of the northern Rust Belt states into low-wage southern states. (The quaint term used for the companies that were relocating was *runaway shops*.) And as we've seen, employers disinvested from high-paying industrial jobs and reinvested instead in low-paying, nonunionized service-sector jobs. "Precarious" or "contingent" jobs—temporary, part-time, subcontracted—also multiplied. For the first time since World War II, a generation of young people grew up expecting to be worse off than the one before.

Employers pointed a finger at the labor movement for causing the problems, and as they doubled down on fighting unions, the government helped them do it. In January 1981, just a couple of months before the launch of District 925, President Reagan took office, and in August, he fired more than eleven thousand striking air traffic controllers—a stunning act that signaled the intensification of the antiunion era.

As employers grew bolder and bolder in opposing unions, the National Labor Relations Board served as their cooperative ally. It was illegal for a company to threaten to shut down if a union came in, but even so, such threats became common practice, without effective pushback from the NLRB. It was illegal to fire employees for union activism, but employers fired them anyway. Charges against employers for committing "unfair labor practices" doubled in the 1970s, but employers kept breaking the law and kept getting away with it.

The Equal Employment Opportunity Commission, the leading federal antidiscrimination agency, received 50,000 complaints in its first five years, beginning in 1965. By 1977 it had a backlog of 120,000 cases. Only 11 percent of cases were ever resolved. Under Reagan the agency's funding was slashed, and its backlog ballooned.

In a sign of the times, the Equal Rights Amendment—"Equality of rights under the law shall not be denied or abridged by the United States or by any State on account of sex"—went down. The amendment won bipartisan support in the US Congress and in many state legislatures, but major corporations, along with a lobby led by conservative women, worked hard against it, and it failed to reach the required number of state legislature ratifications by the 1979 deadline.

Employer resistance to unions became ferocious. Back in the 1950s and '60s, employers had viewed unions as a natural part of doing business. By 1980 those days were decisively over. Employers now considered unions an embarrassing sign of failure. Across the country, unions—including our own—slammed up against a wall of management resistance.

Employers had been on to our movement from the very beginning. Early on, long before we started our union, a spokesman for the John Hancock insurance company told a reporter that existing unions had "missed some boats they could have hopped aboard" in organizing office workers, but "I'd have to say that 9 to 5 represents the most serious effort right now." A decade later, Karen told attendees at our summer school that a management consultant had been heard claiming that "it's not so much the major unions . . . that employers should worry about. The most effective right now is District 925." Another agreed: "District 925 is driving companies in the Northeast crazy," he said. "It's been very effective."

Employers were determined to do everything they could to block us. A key part of their strategy was the use of antiunion consulting firms. While at the beginning of the 1970s only a handful of these union-busting firms existed, by the end of the decade there were thousands. Union busting became a growth industry. "God didn't create unions," said the head of one of the most prominent union-busting firms. "In a normal situation, there aren't any." According to the AFL-CIO, employers hired consultants or lawyers to campaign against the union in nearly three-quarters of union drives.

The consultants designed their strategies with precision. They zeroed in on women's ties to their supervisors and their reluctance to displease their bosses. They stoked women's fears by invoking images of violent conflicts during strikes. They encouraged employees to believe that they would be better off going it alone. Consultants even began using literature from our campaigns when instructing managers on how to fight unions, as we learned when we infiltrated their training sessions.

In the fall of 1979, I went undercover to an antiunion seminar in Washington, DC. I wore a conservative gray suit I'd bought at a discount outlet, slathered my face with makeup, and hobbled into the room on high heels. The participants around me, mostly bank managers, spent the day earnestly taking notes on advice such as this: "Pay attention to employees who seem unhappy or unusually social" and "look out for a sense of direction among otherwise aimless employees."

I took notes too, and when we quoted these instructions at our summer school, everyone howled with laughter. But the consultants, and the employers who hired them, were deadly serious. The consultants had a formula and they followed it to the letter. The basics were these:

1. **Delay the election**. File challenges at the NLRB challenging who should be allowed to vote.
2. **Send in the supervisors**. Make sure supervisors know they're not protected by the National Labor Relations Act and can be fired. By law, they can't tell employees not to join the union, but make sure they hold "captive audience" meetings during the workday where they deliver messages like these: "We care about you! Unions are so impersonal, so restrictive! Without a union, you rise up according to your own merit." If supervisors can be induced to cry in front of their underlings, so much the better.
3. **Threaten**. Enclose a note in the pay envelope: "Union dues would reduce this paycheck." "In case of a strike there will be no more paychecks." Raise the possibility of violence.
4. If the union wins the election, **challenge the results**. Refuse to negotiate. Make the union file charges. Delay, delay, delay.
5. After a contract is signed, encourage employees to mount a **decertification campaign** to vote the union out.

Dorine recalled the effect of antiunion consultants in Boston. "I would watch people go from feeling strong and like we need to do something," she said, "to feeling totally terrified, paralyzed. It was psychological warfare."

The pressure got to her too. "I would literally wake up with nightmares, screaming," she said. "I'd be terrified that we were asking people to put their jobs on the line. I knew from direct experience in my own family what it would have meant if my mother had lost her job."

The consultants tried to capitalize on what they considered the special attributes of women—their compassion, their empathy—and to use those characteristics to build women's sympathy for supervisors and bosses and antipathy for the union. For our part, we sought to turn that compassion toward other office workers and to make use of women's ability to work together harmoniously. Since the consultants counted on secrecy, we publicized their tactics far and wide, warning employees ahead of time about what to expect. All of that helped—but only so much.

Our campaign at the Equitable Life Assurance Society is a case in point—an illustration of creative organizing coming up against enormous obstacles.

Early in 1981 a call came in from a woman who worked at the Syracuse, New York, branch of Equitable. She'd seen a report on TV about District 925 and decided we were exactly what she and her coworkers were looking for. They were a hundred women, most of them in their twenties and thirties. Their primary complaint was that when computers were brought in to replace their typewriters, along with the new machines came a heavier workload, strict monitoring for "quality assurance," and a new salary system that linked raises to rigid production standards. Since the managers didn't understand the new machines, the women had to figure out how to use them and train one another—for no extra pay. They were at their wits' end—yet their managers didn't seem to care. "Any stress is self-imposed," management declared.

We were eager to help these women. Equitable was a huge, powerful company with offices all over the country, and this might have suggested that it was beyond our capabilities. But there were reasons why it was a strategic target. Equitable had a reputation as a progressive company. Coy Eklund, the CEO, was widely admired for speaking out against race and sex discrimination. His public support of women's rights had won him awards and made him something of a darling of the women's movement. As we'd learned in our 9 to 5 organizing, an insurance company's image is all important. We dared to hope that the company might be open to our union. It didn't quite turn out that way.

Cheryl went straight to Syracuse, and a majority of the employees quickly signed union cards. But Equitable pushed back. A consulting firm arrived to enlist the supervisors—most of whom were women and many of whom had close ties with their supervisees—as the frontline troops against the union, charged with assessing pro- or antiunion sentiment in every employee and making sure that as many of them as possible voted no.

The election was held in February 1982, and the union won, 49 to 40. When the votes were counted, many supervisors wept openly.

But winning the election was only the beginning of the struggle. Management challenged the election results at the regional office of the National Labor Relations Board, and when that didn't work, the company filed an appeal with NLRB headquarters in Washington, DC. Meanwhile, they refused to come to the bargaining table.

In June 1982 the national headquarters of the NLRB ruled for the union, but Equitable refused to come to the table. In October the NLRB issued yet another ruling in the union's favor, but still the company wouldn't bargain. Although the NLRB has the power to seek a federal court order to force an employer to bargain, in this case the agency did not.

To combat the company's aggressive stance, we got aggressive too. Using both our 9 to 5 network and SEIU's locals across the country, we passed out flyers in scores of cities with a two-point message, demanding that Equitable not only come to the bargaining table in Syracuse but also stop selling discriminatory insurance policies nationwide. Like many in the insurance industry, Equitable had a long history of charging women customers more than men for the same coverage. By adding pressure from disgruntled female policyholders to the mix, we hoped to bring the company to the bargaining table. It wasn't enough.

In November 1982 SEIU put its muscle to use by calling on members of its New York locals to demonstrate in front of Eklund's office in New York City. A thousand people showed up on their lunch hour with placards that read, WOULD THE REAL COY EKLUND PLEASE STAND UP? (This was a reference to the TV game show *To Tell the Truth*.)

But the company still wouldn't bargain. The next month, in December 1982, SEIU's executive board passed a resolution calling on all its locals to stop doing business with Equitable. No more Equitable health and life insurance benefits. No more using Equitable as an investment manager. A boycott is not a tactic that unions undertake lightly. It was a major step.

Still no progress. Under the National Labor Relations Act, companies were legally barred from closing a workplace in response to a union drive. Nonetheless, in February 1983, Equitable announced plans to close the Syracuse office. The NLRB did nothing.

Say it loud! Karen helped to lead the lunchtime march to bring the insurance company to the bargaining table. *Walter P. Reuther Library, Archives of Labor and Urban Affairs, Wayne State University*

In March the AFL-CIO, which managed more than a billion dollars in union pension funds, announced it was joining the boycott. Unions that belonged to the federation began announcing that they were ending their involvement with Equitable. By February 1984 SEIU reported in its newsletter that the boycott had cost the company millions of dollars. Meanwhile, we were writing to women's rights organizations that had touted Coy Eklund as a friend, and to foundations on whose boards Eklund served, informing them of Equitable's intransigence.

Finally, all the pressure had its intended effect. The company came to the table at last, and bargaining began. In November 1984, two and a half years after we'd won the election, a three-year contract was signed covering just fifty-four employees. It provided for raises of 14 percent, a grievance procedure, and an array of provisions to alleviate the stress of computer work, including extra breaks, an easing of the monitoring program, glare-reduction devices on the screens, adjustable chairs, and the right to transfer away from computer work during pregnancy. The company also agreed not to delay future union elections or bargaining, not to hire any more antiunion consultants, and to keep the office open during the life of the contract.

It was a good contract, the first ever to cover salaried employees at Equitable. It was an enormous breakthrough that sent shock waves throughout the insurance industry and made national news. But at the end of the contract period in 1987, the company closed the Syracuse office and laid off all the employees.

Was all of this a sign that unionizing office workers in the finance industries might just be too difficult?

Maybe so. When our organizing took off in the Midwest and in Seattle, it was not in the finance industries and not in the private sector where we'd expected it, but in the public sector, in county government, in government-run Head Start preschool programs, and at public libraries, colleges, and universities. Previously, public employees' unions had been illegal in many places. But by the 1970s, the laws had changed, and public-sector unionizing had begun to flourish. Once we had a base in the public sector, like other unions that were organizing clericals, we figured we could circle back around to the private sector.

Not that organizing in the public sector was a piece of cake.

At the Cuyahoga County Public Library, negotiating came to a dead halt over the issue of pay. One evening, at a meeting of the union negotiating committee, everyone was in despair.

"When are they going to give in?" one member moaned.

"Not till the cows come home," another answered bitterly.

Library workers may have an image as quiet introverts who care mostly about shushing noisy patrons, but these staffers turned out to have their goofy side.

"Moooove on wages," someone boomed.

The room cracked up, and within a couple of days a herd of plastic cows appeared on the lawn of the library administration building. To get to their monthly public meeting, members of the board of trustees had to walk a gauntlet of a hundred workers ringing cowbells and grinning from ear to ear. A successful contract soon followed.

Our drive at nearby Cuyahoga Community College, the largest community college in Ohio, began in 1981 when the administration made employees reapply for their own jobs and then turned many of them down. Here one of the biggest challenges was to overcome racial divisions within the workforce. Tri-C, as it was known, had three separate campuses. The downtown Metropolitan campus had mostly Black students and staff, the Western campus had mostly White employees, and the Eastern campus was integrated. Employees at one campus tended not to know their counterparts at the other two.

To overcome these obstacles, we built a fifty-person organizing committee made up of employees from all three campuses. As in all our drives, our leadership team was as diverse as the workforce itself. It had to be. You can't win a union election without reaching out to every part of the workforce.

At times, some of the employees at the mostly White campus were hesitant to speak with a Black staffer. "They said everything *but*, 'We want a White organizer,'" remembered Carol Sims. "They were tough." But she kept meeting with them. "They were poor, struggling women trying to make a living," said Jackie Harris, a Black clerical worker who became the president of the union at the college. "They wanted raises, and they wanted better working conditions too."

We took deliberate steps to bring together young and old, White people and people of color, men and women. By targeting the boss and working together for a common purpose, people of diverse backgrounds gained power together. The recognition of common problems and common goals was key to the union victory in 1982.

One more thing about Tri-C: many of the employees were part-timers, and as at many workplaces, management wanted to exclude them from the union. We didn't see it that way. "I don't know if it was our ignorance or what," Bonnie remembered, "but it was one of those times where we just thought, 'We can do this if we set our minds to it.' And we did it." The part-timers became union members.

In 1984, after the Ohio legislature granted the right to bargain over wages and benefits, members of the clerical staff committee at the University of Cincinnati began interviewing unions, looking for the best fit for the university's fourteen hundred office workers. District 925 was their choice. For employees who felt they were regularly put down on the job, our union was a breath of fresh air—a place that took them seriously and helped them develop strategies for winning the job improvements they were after.

"We had been told so long that we weren't important and so nearly invisible that we all started to believe it," said Carolyn Schwier, who became the union president at the university. "And then 925 came in and started telling us that we were important and that we had a lot of power if we joined together and used it. The union coached me and made me stretch and take on things I hadn't thought I could do."

"In the union," said Valarie Long, "I learned the craft of organizing. I learned to count, and I learned to listen. It was a transformative experience for me." She went on to become an executive vice president of SEIU nationwide.

As the drive got underway, there were petitions, postcards, and posters. Union supporters wore buttons reading WE ARE THE POWER. One day they all wore red. Prounion workers could spot one another across the room and feel encouraged, and people who were unsure could see that their coworkers were for the union and not afraid to say so. A subtle shift in the office culture took hold. Employees began to understand that being outspoken might get them places that being quiet and "ladylike" had not. Nobody got fired, and employees began to see that the more visible you were, the safer you were.

The administration's law firm mounted an intensive effort to defeat the union drive, holding mandatory department-by-department meetings in which office workers were "educated" about why unions were a bad idea. Supervisors also called in employees individually to enlighten them about the downsides of a union. We lost the first election in 1986 by 29 votes out of 1,400.

After that loss, the university slashed benefits and cut back on raises, and a second union drive started up. This time, in October 1988, we won the vote by a two-to-one margin and bargained a first contract. But after that contract expired, the university once again tried to squeeze the clericals by attempting to take back much of what had been won. The administration offered three years without raises, less sick leave, and an end to the tuition remission program under which employees had access to university courses.

In response, in 1992 the women came up with a tactic just bold and surprising enough to break through the university's resistance. They called it the "herd."

At exactly 10:00 AM, one person in every department stood up and blew a whistle—a real whistle this time, not a metaphorical one as in the days of the anonymous "whistleblowers" at the First National Bank and the John Hancock insurance company. The piercing noise was the signal for everyone to walk out. In most strikes, employees don't show up for work at all, but the herd was different. We wanted the women to be present and together. "Standing up and walking out may not sound so courageous," said Debbie Schneider, who led the drive and later became the national president of District 925. But it was. The workers who walked out had to assert themselves in front of their bosses, their coworkers, and the students and others they interacted with. Once out of the buildings, they formed a parade that snaked through the campus—a "herd" of hundreds of workers, all handing out flyers and rattling soda cans filled with beans. The parade stretched across the campus, and the cans made a terrific din.

Office workers on the move. *Walter P. Reuther Library, Archives of Labor and Urban Affairs, Wayne State University*

The result was an excellent contract.

At the University of Washington, the three-thousand-person clerical workforce hadn't received a raise in years when Kim Cook, who'd started as a member of Seattle 9 to 5, joined the organizing staff. Kim and her fellow organizers walked their legs off, crisscrossing the campus to talk to as many employees as they could, as often as they could. Bonnie, our West Coast organizer, was her supervisor. Bonnie's mantra was "I refuse to do anything by myself." "My way of operating is always to get a little gang together," Bonnie said. "We figure it out together, because everybody has good ideas, and then I help them do what they don't know how to do."

"Whenever I came to Bonnie with a problem," Kim said, "she always made me try to answer the question first, rather than offering advice." Kim followed Bonnie's model. "I tend to want to tell people what to do, but Bonnie taught me to make people think for themselves. I learned from her to rely on the collective wisdom of the group."

As at Tri-C in Cleveland, in Seattle the racial divisions among the university employees were a challenge. White, Black, Asian, and Latina employees were sometimes hesitant about joining together. But as women of different races found a home in the union, tensions eased.

At the university, as everywhere, our organizing was powered by the ideas of the women's movement, which has sometimes been characterized as exclusively White. It was not our experience, however, that women of color stayed away from the union because they felt alienated from feminism.

Debra Young, a racial justice activist, was among the Black union leaders at the university who believed from the start that the women's movement could only help. "We African Americans could ride on that wave," she said.

Some women of color who didn't identify with the women's movement at first came to embrace it through the union. "Black women have been fighting for equality at work their whole lives," said Gilda Turner, "so I never really took on that label of being a feminist." Once she became involved in the union, though, she came to accept the label. "I kind of had to agree, 'OK, well, maybe I *am* a feminist.'"

In one round of bargaining, the union won renown for our strategic deployment of an "embarrassing" word. All over campus, in a cost-cutting move, management had removed the tampon machines from the women's restrooms. Women were not pleased. Reinstating the machines became a key bargaining point—for two reasons. First, women were truly pissed off that the machines had been taken away. And second, the mere mention of tampons turned out to make members of the management team so uncomfortable that they had to leave the room. That worked to the union's advantage. "Whenever they started saying something awful about wages," one union leader remembered, "we'd bring the conversation back to Tampax."

The machines were reinstated.

We'd vowed to focus on the finance industry, yet employer resistance there and all across the private sector made organizing more difficult than we ever anticipated. We'd predicted a wave of clerical workers joining unions, but the wave was not happening.

Across the country, we had no trouble finding office workers who wanted to unionize, and despite employer resistance we were able to win the great majority of our drives. Once we won an election, though, employers poured so many powerful resources into impeding the negotiations that in our first two years, although we won nine elections covering four thousand workers, we were able to win only six contracts covering a total of eight hundred workers.

We weren't the only union having trouble. Throughout the economy, the labor movement was reeling. As factories closed or moved away, as automation came in, as jobs moved out of heavy industry into the service sector, unions lost members at a massive rate. In 1955 one-third of workers belonged to unions. By 1981, when we launched District 925, less than a quarter did. At the bargaining table, unions had to fight just to hold on to the wages and benefits they'd won in previous contracts. Often they were forced to make big concessions. Nonunion workers watched this happening and became less likely to believe that a union could help them.

As unions struggled with the twin tasks of protecting the dwindling ranks of their existing members *and* recruiting new ones, organizing slowed way down. The year 1981 saw the lowest level of elections in decades. There were fewer wins too. Where in the past most union drives had succeeded, by 1980, most failed. Decertification elections—campaigns to vote out existing unions—rose by 400 percent in ten years, and unions lost 75 percent of them. By the late 1980s, as employer resistance became increasingly effective, one-third of workers who won a union election never got a union, and by the 1990s, only 56 percent of workers who chose a union were able to win a first contract.

By the end of the 1980s, the staff of District 925 was beginning to move on. Jackie left in 1988, and the next year Dorine took a job with the Massachusetts teachers' union. Cheryl became a director of the AIDS Action Committee of Massachusetts. Bonnie began organizing nursing home workers and found that her job became much easier, whether because these employees were more open to unions or because their employers mounted less resistance. "It was just, 'My boss is a jerk—where do I sign?'" she remembered.

In 1993 President Bill Clinton tapped Karen to head the Women's Bureau of the Department of Labor. Debbie Schneider took her place as head of the union, and Ellen Bravo, the director of our Milwaukee chapter, became the national director of 9 to 5.

While many staffers considered 9 to 5 and District 925 to be unusually family friendly, others left when they became mothers. I personally found it difficult to be both a 9 to 5 staffer and a parent. My job as director of our Washington policy office didn't require me to work superlong hours, and as time went by, I ended up spending most of my time in the Philadelphia office. This made it possible to imagine having a baby. But just like for millions of other parents, when my first child was born, the so-called work-family dilemma landed in my lap.

For Jeff and me, being parents together deepened our connection and brought us much joy. It also opened up new areas of conflict. Before the baby was born, we agreed that we would split the parenting duties fifty-fifty. That turned out to be harder than expected. As my three months of maternity leave came to an end, to my surprise I couldn't imagine enrolling our son in all-day day care, as we'd planned. Jeff loved the baby to pieces but felt fine about having him cared for by others. I felt deeply torn. I loved 9 to 5. I didn't want to leave my job. But I loved the baby and couldn't get enough of him. I loved carrying him around. Gazing into his face. Feeding him. Listening to him coo. Coaxing him to smile. Watching him sleep.

Maybe if our society had had a different approach to early parenthood—longer paid leave for new parents and widely available excellent day care, for starters—things would have been different. Maybe not. For a while I tried to emulate Karen and other staffers who seemed not to skip a beat as they added parenting to their job responsibilities. They brought their babies along with them to meetings or left them with caregivers, and it seemed to work for them. But for me it all seemed more difficult.

I tried bringing the baby to the office and parking him in a bouncy seat next to my desk. At midday Jeff would come and take the baby back to his office for a few hours. That arrangement lasted for a week or two before it proved unworkable. Next I teamed up with a friend, and together we hired a babysitter to care for both of our babies at once. That went well. But overnight meetings of our national staff posed a challenge. When our son was six or seven months old, I brought him with me to one of these meetings in Cleveland (airplane, diaper bag, borrowed portacrib) and dropped him off for the day with a local woman who cared for several children in her home. When I showed up at five o'clock, my son was lying on his back in the middle of the floor, staring at the ceiling. I was horrified. He *never* just lay on the floor staring at the ceiling. A few months later, I brought him with me to a conference in Boston and left him with a babysitter provided by the hotel. I dimly remember a disaster with pureed sweet potatoes and a shag rug. For the next overnight meeting in Cleveland, I left him home with Jeff and rented an electric breast pump to carry with me on the plane. The businessman in the next seat raised an eyebrow as I stowed the heavy leather case under the seat. "Office machine," I muttered.

These arrangements worked out, some better than others, but when our daughter was born a few years later, I had a hard time imagining doing it all again. After much agonizing, I left the 9 to 5 staff and started working from home as a speechwriter for our parent union, SEIU. In addition to coauthoring two books for 9 to 5 (*9 to 5: The Working Woman's Guide to Office Survival* and *The 9 to 5 Guide to Combating Sexual Harassment*), I went on to do other kinds of writing. I wrote articles for women's magazines and a column on "work from the worker's point of view" for

the *Philadelphia Daily News*. I was a speechwriter in the Clinton administration. I wrote a play about my Aunt Jessie (a longtime secretary, the
one who wore her hair in a Jane Fonda shag in the nursing home), which
became a film called *Beautiful Hills of Brooklyn*. I wrote a book called *We
Are Here: Memories of the Lithuanian Holocaust*, about how people were
facing the past in the land where my grandfather was born. I became a
literary translator from Yiddish. My career has taken me to a wide variety of places, but to my mind it all fits together. I know for certain that
everything I learned in my years with 9 to 5, and all the growing up I
did in the organization, was vitally important in shaping what came after.

––––––––––

At the end of the 1990s, SEIU began to change its structure, consolidating
locals in order to maximize resources and power. Throughout the union,
meetings were held to figure out how to group similar types of workers
together to create much bigger units. In this new scenario, District 925, with
our ten thousand members, was not considered large enough to stand on
its own, especially since our members were spread out all over the country,
in Boston, Cleveland, Cincinnati, and Seattle.

In 1999 several dozen District 925 staff and leaders from across the
country assembled at a retreat—a convent in Kentucky, not far from Cincinnati—to discuss the future of the union. It was an emotional meeting.
No one wanted to see the end of our woman-run union. No one wanted
to lose the connections that had been forged from coast to coast. But by
all rational measures, the breakup of District 925 made sense, and most
members came to feel that the reorganization was for the best.

By June 2001 the new structure was in place. Our members in Ohio
joined an SEIU local that grew to 27,000 members. Our 1,500 members in
the Boston area, mostly public employees who worked at schools, libraries, and government offices, were distributed among several SEIU locals.
The Seattle local, home of the University of Washington clericals, kept
the name "Local 925," and Kim Cook was elected president. The local
conducted an election for 10,000 childcare providers and won with over
90 percent of the vote. It was a new arena for organizing and a landmark
win. In time, the local grew to encompass 24,000 members. So although

District 925 as a nationwide entity was no more, the name "925" survived and flourished.

In myriad ways, District 925 was a stunning success. We built a 10,000-member union from scratch. Within our first two years, we won nine elections involving 4,000 workers, with twelve other drives in progress. Our win rate was about 85 percent—as good as or better than any other local in our parent union. We added 10 percent to our membership rolls every year, and we won great contracts.

"No matter how difficult things got, we all kept our sense of humor and moved forward like warriors," one of our leaders recalled. "I'm very proud of that."

Our spirit couldn't be beat. We had high expectations for ourselves and for one another. We weren't working for personal glory. We were all in this together, working for a cause. Carol Sims put it succinctly: "It's the jazz of it—the jazz of winning. Once you win one campaign and you get that under your belt, you think you can conquer the world."

At the SEIU conventions that took place every four years, the District 925 women always came in bursting with pride. One year we marched in carrying flags, each one representing a place we'd organized. "We strode into that convention," one member remembered, "and we were nothing but banners."

15

LOOKING BACK,
LOOKING AHEAD

WHAT DID WE ACHIEVE? What did we fail to achieve?

Starting in Boston and spreading across the country, our movement brought people together across race and class and changed the lives of working women everywhere. With surveys and hotlines, leaflets and petitions, rallies and lobbying, meetings and public gatherings, hearings and discrimination charges, contests and press releases and antics of all kinds, we took on the most powerful companies in the land. We won millions of dollars in back pay and raises, improvements in hiring and training, and career ladders that enabled women and people of color to move into higher-paying jobs. We made workplaces run better, to the benefit of women and men alike. We embarrassed bosses, scared them, educated them, pressured them until they made the changes we were demanding. And we made them make their own coffee. Today when you look back at the way offices used to function, the stereotyped images of working women at the beginning of our journey seem outdated—and, well, bizarre.

We got government moving on our behalf. We pushed for stronger enforcement of antidiscrimination regulations and helped make sexual harassment and pregnancy discrimination illegal. We blew the whistle on wage-fixing. As automation transformed America's offices, we developed bargaining points and legislation to protect the health and the rights of office workers.

We made clear that women's problems at work were not just personal matters but matters of policy, collective issues that unions and policy makers could help to resolve.

Just like during earlier eras in American labor history, in the 1970s and '80s women were at the forefront of the fight for rights on the job. We brought new energy and new ideas into the union movement. Venturing beyond the workplace-by-workplace approach that was standard at the time, we operated industry-wide and citywide. We used the momentum of the women's movement to attract members from workplaces big and small, whether they were ready for a union or not. We harnessed the power of the hullabaloo to tremendous effect.

We and other worker activists of the 1970s, according to historian Dorothy Sue Cobble, "expanded the vocabulary of workplace rights, made a public and political issue of the gendered construction of women's jobs, and invented new forms of workplace representation." In the words of historian Linda Gordon, the uprising of women in the 1970s, of which we were a part, "wrought massive change."

We developed a generation of committed activists who made their mark wherever they went. A few examples: after heading the Women's Bureau of the Department of Labor and the Working Women's Department of the AFL-CIO, Karen Nussbaum went on to found Working America, the community arm of the AFL-CIO. With millions of members, Working America became one of the nation's biggest and most far-reaching organizations for working women and men.

After serving as president of District 925 until it was absorbed into other locals, Debbie Schneider became the director of SEIU's global organizing program.

After heading Local 925 in Seattle and helping to bring thousands of childcare workers into the union, Kim Cook worked in leadership development at SEIU's Washington headquarters, then became a labor educator at the Cornell Worker Institute in New York City.

Michelle Healy became a long-term SEIU organizer. "I thought of 9 to 5 recently," she wrote in 2021, "when fast food workers walked off the job in Sacramento in July after days without air conditioning. The boss told them the air conditioning was working fine—they must just be menopausal. The fight for justice is still going on!"

Other 9 to 5 leaders would become leaders in government, health care, and other endeavors. Ellen Bravo started a coalition called Family Values @ Work and wrote two books—*The Job/Family Challenge: A 9 to 5 Guide* and *Taking on the Big Boys: Or Why Feminism Is Good for Families, Business, and the Nation*. Others went on to fill such positions as regional director for a governor, community relations director for a public hospital, director of a city health care program for the homeless, creator of career programs for low-wage workers, chief of staff for a state legislator, adviser on women's issues for a mayor, policy director for the speaker of a statehouse, occupational health professional, instructor in English as a second language, minister, and trainer of people with disabilities seeking to enter the workforce. One former staffer spoke for many when she said, "What I learned in the 9 to 5 movement—planning a meeting, leadership development, writing and communication, organizing, developing campaigns—I put to use wherever I go."

In our dreams, the decade of the 1980s was to be a time of union organizing wins and bargaining victories on a historic scale. It turned out not to be.

Instead, all across America, the labor movement suffered a steep decline. By 2021 fewer than 11 percent of workers were union members. That included 7 percent of private-sector workers and a little less than 35 percent of public-sector workers. It was as low a percentage as in the 1930s, before the passage of the National Labor Relations Act. Among office and administrative support workers, 10 percent were represented by unions. Black workers continued to be more likely to be union members than White, Asian, or Latino workers.

By the turn of the twenty-first century, work in America had changed enormously. The gig economy took off. For many people, the term "9 to 5" no longer described the hours of the workday. More workers were required to be on call around the clock. People had to patch together two or three jobs in order to put food on the table. An average worker worked two hundred hours more each year in 2000 compared to 1973. As the economy began to recover from the Great Recession of 2007, temporary employment grew four times faster than overall US employment. Fewer workers had job-based health benefits, pensions, sick days, or vacation time. By 2021 about 30 percent of full-time workers lacked employer-paid health insurance and about 40 percent didn't have pensions.

Pay took a huge hit. Earlier, as productivity went up, pay rose too. From 1948 to 1973, productivity went up by 96.7 percent, and pay kept pace, rising by 91.3 percent. But starting in 1973, that pattern went out the window. From 1973 to 2013, productivity rose 74.4 percent, but wages rose only 9.2 percent. Beginning in the 1970s, income inequality began to soar to the point where it approached the extremes of the period just before the Great Depression. In 1965 CEOs made twenty-four times more than the average production worker. By 2009 they made 185 times more.

As for the wage gap between men and women, during most of the twentieth century, the average woman earned about 60 percent of the average man's wage—sometimes a bit more, sometimes a bit less. (Hence the green buttons I remember from the 1970s that said simply 59 CENTS.) Beginning in the late 1970s, the gender gap in pay narrowed substantially, with women coming to earn about 80 percent of what men earned. But this historic rise slowed down on the way to equality, and by 2005, progress came to a halt. By 2021 the figure hadn't budged.

The wage gap stems in part from occupational segregation. Just like in the early 1970s, people of different sexes and races continue to work in different jobs. Although women are a little less than half (47 percent) of the workforce, they fill about two-thirds of the low-wage jobs. Most of the highest-paying occupations are predominantly male, while most of the lowest-paying occupations are predominantly female. Male-dominated jobs tend to pay more than female-dominated jobs, even when the jobs require equal levels of education, skill, and responsibility. When women of different races are in the same jobs, they appear to earn about the same pay. But women of color are more likely to work in low-wage jobs. Today Black women earn on average 63 percent of the pay of White men, and Latina women 55 percent.

Workplace discrimination continues. About four in ten working women report facing workplace discrimination because of their sex. One in four say they've earned less than a man doing the same job. Women are penalized for having to care for children and for being "aggressive" or "persistent"—qualities that employers prize in men. In 2021 one in four Black and Latino employees reported having been discriminated against at work within the previous year. Workers continue to be harassed for their sexual orientation. And as the baby boomer generation grows old, age discrimination—unequal treatment of workers ages forty and over, which is prohibited by law—is among the fastest-growing kinds of workplace discrimination. Older job seekers find it harder to get hired, and many face pressure to retire before they're ready.

In offices women make up 73 percent of office and administrative support workers. Within these jobs, 77 percent of workers are White and 14 percent are Black.

Although office work continues to be central to the economy, job growth in the office sector began to slow by the early 1980s. The impact of new technology on the number of office jobs has been mixed. Some-how, men learned to type and more bosses began handling clerical tasks. By 2015, there were half as many secretaries as in 1979. But not all clerical jobs took a hit. You might have expected that as ATMs came into widespread usage, the number of bank tellers would go down. In fact, however, the number of bank tellers held steady and even increased. Tellers now handle more complex tasks, though not always with an increase in pay.

In place of jobs that were phased out, other kinds of office jobs were created. The good news is that some of these new jobs involve creativity and problem-solving skills, and some pay better. But despite the promise that the new technology would eliminate tedium, some of the new office jobs are heavily routinized and more monotonous than ever before—and poorly paid.

Since our movement began, management jobs have opened up for women. Starting in the 1960s, women in general and Black women in particular began moving into management, professional, and technical occupations in great numbers. But just as with the narrowing of the wage gap, progress in the opening up of top jobs began to slow in the 1980s. In 1970 census data showed that one in six American managers was a woman. Fifty years later, somewhat more than two in five managers were women—progress, but not yet equality. Disappointingly, while our movement fought to create career paths so that those in the lowest jobs could make their way up the ladder, that goal has not been realized. As jobs for women opened up at the higher levels of the office hierarchy, women in the lowest-paying jobs tended not to be promoted into those jobs. The economic divide between women in lower-skilled jobs and those in higher-skilled jobs grew wider.

The COVID-19 pandemic took a toll on women and people of color in particular. Pay for CEOs continued to rise during the pandemic, but pay for the average worker did not. Millions of women left the workforce. Women, especially women of color, were more likely than men to be laid off or fired. Some women left their jobs to take care of their children when schools closed down.

———————

The struggle for rights and respect, empowerment and equality goes on. Unions remain among the most powerful tools for closing the pay gap and guaranteeing equal pay. Unionized women earn an average of 12.9 percent more than their nonunion counterparts, and they're much more likely to have job-based health insurance and a retirement plan. But new strategies will be needed to meet the challenges facing the women workers of the future. Questions that remain to be answered include these:

- How can workers overcome the weakness of the labor laws and the decline of union membership?
- What power can workers wield in the new economy?
- What will convince women workers by the millions to engage in collective action?
- What kinds of organizations will women workers be most inclined to join?

The new generation of women helping to lead the labor movement will be key to answering these questions. Since our movement began, the AFL-CIO and many of the largest unions have come to be headed by women. Under John Sweeney's leadership, the AFL-CIO expanded its Executive Council to bring in more women and people of color. In 2021 Liz Shuler was elected president of the AFL-CIO, the first woman to hold that position. Fred Redmond of the United Steelworkers was elected as secretary-treasurer, the first Black person to hold the number two office. Along with executive vice president Tefere Gebre, the first immigrant in the position, they made up the most diverse team of officers in the federation's history.

Shuler calls the AFL-CIO, with its 6.5 million women members, "the largest working women's organization in the country." If current trends continue, women will become a majority of the unionized workforce. Interviewed after her election, Shuler said, "I intend to stand on the shoulders of those giants, the women who have come before me, the women who have led those strikes and are on the picket lines, and also the quiet strength of women in the workplace who have been leaders in every workplace around our great country."

In 2017 Mary Kay Henry became the president of SEIU. In 2021 only one of seven national SEIU officers was a White male, and women ran most of the departments at the union's headquarters. Becky Pringle became the head of the National Education Association. Randi Weingarten headed the American Federation of Teachers. Elissa McBride was the vice president of AFSCME. Sara Nelson, the president of the Association of Flight Attendants, affiliated with the CWA, was a prominent voice; her slogan, directed at women, was "Join unions, run unions."

Today workers increasingly say they want to belong to a union. Forty-eight percent of nonunion workers in a 2018 survey said they would join a union if they could. But there's no denying that unions remain out of reach for most workers. With the weakening of labor laws over the years, 90 percent of worker attempts to get a union contract do not succeed when employers put up resistance.

Some union organizing today takes place in the traditional mode within the rubric of the National Labor Relations Act. In this scenario, employees at a particular workplace get together to gather union cards, vote in an election overseen by the National Labor Relations Board, and bargain for a contract. Examples abound. Beginning in the

1990s, OPEIU conducted successful organizing drives in the insurance industry. The UAW is a longtime leader in campus organizing. The Teamsters Union represents tens of thousands of office workers in thirty-three states and continues to organize clericals. In May 2021 AFSCME won a first contract for twenty thousand state employees in Nevada, and in July 2021, in partnership with SEIU, AFSCME bargained a first contract covering forty thousand family childcare providers in California.

Other kinds of organizing fall into a category known as *alt-labor.* Taxi drivers, restaurant workers, home care workers, day laborers, freelancers, and other kinds of workers are experimenting—just as 9 to 5 has done—with a variety of strategies *not* based in the traditional mode. Just as we in 9 to 5 built on the momentum of the women's movement, today's worker initiatives are gaining strength from the immigration and racial justice movements.

SEIU has broken new ground with its Justice for Janitors campaign. Instead of organizing and bargaining workplace by workplace, the campaign targets the entire cleaning industry in a particular city all at once, and the resulting master contract applies to janitors throughout the city. The effort began in 1990 with a citywide strike in Los Angeles that resulted in a 22 percent raise over three years for janitors across the city. The movement then spread to Houston, Miami, and Boston, and came to include more than 225,000 janitors in nearly thirty cities in the United States and four in Canada.

SEIU's "Fight for $15" campaign is another alt-labor initiative that reaches out to growing areas of the workforce including childcare and other home care workers, fast-food workers, airport workers, convenience store workers, and more. It began in 2012 when a group of McDonald's workers walked off the job in New York City. The campaign pressures states, cities, and counties to raise the minimum wage for all area employees. It has benefited twenty-six million people—nearly 16 percent of the US workforce—including nearly twelve million workers of color and eighteen million women. As the campaign's leaders put it, workers "come together and act like a union" to win their demands. Actual union membership comes later.

An effort headed by the National Domestic Workers Alliance advocates for the rights of nearly 2.5 million nannies, house cleaners, and home care workers. The group has won a Domestic Workers Bill of Rights in a dozen cities and states. The coalition called Family Values @ Work presses states and local jurisdictions to require sick days and paid leave for workers who are ill or caring for new babies or other family members. Coworker.org supports employees in a wide variety of workplaces in pressing for better working conditions.

New strategies are also being pioneered in the tech sector, the big-box companies, and the warehouses that occupy a greater part of the economy than ever before. In 2020 the Communications Workers of America formed the Campaign to Organize Digital Employees (CODE-CWA), a network of workers in the tech, game, and digital industries, with members at major multinational companies and tiny start-ups alike. CWA also continues to be a leader in representing workers at customer call centers. Organizations such as United for Respect and One Fair Wage advocate for higher pay and better working conditions at the nation's largest retailers and small businesses alike.

Since its creation in 2013, the woman-initiated Black Lives Matter movement has voiced demands for racial justice across the country. The #MeToo movement against sexual harassment gained nationwide visibility in 2017 and got a boost in 2019 when UNITE HERE, the hotel and hospitality union, mobilized bartenders, servers, and room attendants—mostly women of color—to take on a powerful hotel chain to win "panic buttons" for housekeepers to protect them against harassment.

Half a century after it was founded, 9 to 5 is still a national organization active in every state. The group has broadened its goals beyond office workers. It focuses on supporting legislation for paid sick leave, parental leave, childcare, equal pay, and an end to discrimination. In 2021 the group sponsored a cross-country bus tour in support of a federal paid leave policy. It also hosts forums on affordable childcare and helps renters facing eviction to find legal assistance.

Contact 9to5.org. *9to5, National Association of Working Women*

In the early years of our movement, I sat on a bluff looking up at a sky full of puffy clouds and contemplated the question of the "duck and the wave." What if we activists were nothing more than "ducks" floating on the surface of the water, propelled by great economic and social forces over which we had no control? Could I or any of us really hope to influence the course of history?

Back then, I recalled what Robert F. Kennedy said—about how each of us contributes a "tiny ripple of hope," and about how, "from a million different centers of energy and daring, those ripples build a current that can sweep down the mightiest walls of oppression and resistance." Those words help me to know that we did make a difference.

I'm proud of what we did. We won a lot. Our hopes and dreams were huge; we didn't win it all. In this line of work, you're always reaching for the horizon and beyond. You're never satisfied. You never achieve everything you try for. Your victories along the way only whet your appetite for more.

There's much more to do. Isn't that the way it always goes? The song "Pass It On" says:

> Freedom, freedom is a hard-won thing
> You've got to work for it, fight for it
> Day and night for it
> And every generation's got to win it again

EPILOGUE

In 2021 on September 25 ("9/25"—get it?), we 9 to 5'ers gathered for a reunion. Because of the pandemic, the gathering was partly in person in Washington, DC, and partly virtual. There were masks, hugs and virtual hugs, singing and dancing, smiles and tears, and old photos.

Karen took us back to the beginning. "At our very first meeting in Boston in 1973," she said, "when I looked out at a room full of 150 secretaries, I knew we were on to something."

We had been indeed. Together, we shared our memories of the funniest, the hardest, and the proudest moments.

Of course, it wouldn't have been a 9 to 5 event without a survey, and this one was no exception. Among the questions posed were these: What do you have to say to today's activists and organizers? What do women need to do today to win rights and respect? Here's a sample of what we answered:

Have fun. Be creative.

Approach the problem as systemic, not individual. Collective action and solutions are key.

Remember that the goal is power-building.

Talk to your coworkers, be ready with workable solutions, then collectively bring issues to decision makers. Most importantly, don't accept no for an answer!

Focus on lifting the floor, not just the ceiling.

Decelerate. Do everything in the time it takes, not necessarily at the speed of light.

Take care of each other.

Never give up. Even your losses will help you win in the future.

Remember the heroes who paved the way in the struggles that came before.

Always remember sisterhood and solidarity, especially in the face of sexism, racism, and other forms of hatred.

We are what we were. We all carry the ideas and experiences of those who came before.

We will not have a just and sustainable economy until we eradicate the long-standing inequities deeply woven into the fibers of our economy, in which some jobs are still undervalued based on the color of our skin or our gender.

Remember there is strength in numbers. Find common ground. Challenge the bosses for a say over your job, your community, your country, your democracy.

Reach out to another woman out of your comfort zone—she's been waiting for you!

Keep telling the 9 to 5 story.

Educate your children, your family, and your friends about the crucial role that labor has in saving the world from climate disaster and poverty.

Vote!

The fight is never over, because it's always about power: who has it, who doesn't, who needs it and how they get it. Never pass up an opportunity to organize.

And finally:

Frankly, I don't think the younger generation needs my advice. There are some amazing organizers out there.

As for me and Jeff, after a lifetime together, we're still going strong. Our children are grown, with families of their own.

Throughout my years in the working women's movement, I carried a vivid picture in my head of someday telling my grandchildren all about 9 to 5. I still have that picture in my head, and I know I will tell them all about it when they're old enough. But of course, I'm not satisfied with telling *just* my grandchildren. Hence this book.

My hope is that the story of the 9 to 5 women—our story, my story—will inspire a new generation to link arms and join together for rights and respect on the job. I hope new generations will be "touched by fire," as we were. And just as we learned from those who came before but went on to forge our own path, I hope those who come after us will do the same.

ACKNOWLEDGMENTS

My greatest debt is to the countless women workers, both those I knew and those I didn't, who through their bravery, passion, determination, and humor helped to change the work world for millions.

Jerome Pohlen and his team at Chicago Review Press, including Frances Giguette and Elizabeth Yellen, were unfailingly professional and a pleasure to work with.

Jennifer Lyons and her team were fierce and energetic advocates.

I can't adequately express my gratitude to my friends and colleagues in the 9 to 5 movement, especially Karen Nussbaum and Janet Selcer, for all that they did and all that they do. They provided many wonderful kinds of support during the writing, as did Kim Cook, Debbie Schneider, and Pat Thomas. I thank Ellen Bravo, Leng Leng Chancey, Nancy Farrell, Jackie Harris, Anne Hill, Mary Jung, Dorine Levasseur, Valarie Long, Carolyn Schwier, Carol Sims, Diane Teichert, Gilda Turner, and Debra Young for their help as well.

I will always be grateful to the late John J. Sweeney. I thank Liz Shuler of the AFL-CIO and Mary Kay Henry of the Service Employees International Union. Elissa McBride and Dalia Thornton generously filled me in on the activities of the American Federation of State, County, and Municipal Employees. Phil Kugler, David Kusnet, and Tish Olshefski provided information on the activities of the American Federation of Teachers. For information on the activities of the Communications Workers of America,

I thank Larry Cohen, Debbie Goldman, and George Kohl. Vicki Saporta, Sara Payne, Brian Alde, Rome Aloise, Matt Metcalf, and Jason Rabinowitz provided information on the activities of the International Brotherhood of Teamsters. Julie Kushner talked with me about the activities of District 65 and the United Auto Workers.

Both for crucial insights about the work and for sustaining support, I'm grateful to Mary Carpenter, Morayo Faleyimu, Sarah Glazer, Jackie Kendall, Susannah O'Donnell, Penny Sablove, Meg Samuels, Mimi Schwartz, and Natalie Wexler. I thank Peter Dreier and Molly Schultz Hafid for their help.

Julia Reichert and Steven Bognar—filmmakers extraordinaire—pointed the way forward in their splendid documentary *9to5: The Story of a Movement*. They continue to inspire me as model storytellers, change makers, artists, and human beings. Their teammates Ben Evory, Cait Rowe, and Crystal Whetstone provided invaluable support and research. I thank Camille Hardman and Gary Lane for telling the 9 to 5 story in their sparkling film *Still Working 9 to 5*.

Lane Windham, author of *Knocking on Labor's Door*, helped to educate me about the US economy and about the archival research I needed to do. Her insights about the 9 to 5 movement were transformative for me.

I am grateful to the staff of several libraries, especially the Schlesinger Library of the Harvard Radcliffe Institute, where archives of the 9 to 5 organization can be found, and the Walter P. Reuther Library, Archives of Labor and Urban Affairs, at Wayne State University, where archives of both 9 to 5 and District 925 can be found. Sarah Lebovitz and Stefanie Caloia were particularly helpful. I thank Ann Froines for the invaluable interviews she conducted, which are available at Wayne State. I also thank the staff at the libraries of the University of Illinois Chicago, the Chicago History Museum, and Cleveland State University. (Special thanks to Beth Piwkowski.)

I am grateful to the Cenacle Retreat and Conference Center in Chicago, and especially to Crystal Chan. Richard Bermack, Steve Cagan, Nancy Farrell, and Nasreen Jilani generously helped with photos.

Anne Dubuisson and Ken Krimstein helped me make my way through the publication process. Their warmth and friendship helped me sleep at night.

Heather Booth and Steve Max, my teachers at the Midwest Academy, have been important stars in my firmament for half a century. I'm grateful to Richard Aregood for hiring me, way back when, to write a column about "work from the worker's point of view" for the *Philadelphia Daily News*.

I am deeply grateful to my parents, who helped to make me who I am as a writer and an activist. My siblings, my children, my in-laws, and my grandchildren give meaning to my life every day, as do dear friends—Susan, Jodi, Jessica, Ahron, Dick, Nancy, Laura, Jim, and the members of my Yiddish reading circle.

Looking back at this formative time in my life was an intense and fascinating process that changed me in important ways. I thank Shira Karman for an illuminating conversation about my struggle to be both a girlfriend and an organizer.

Finally, I thank Jeff Blum for being my beloved life partner—my friend, my beacon, my steady light.

TIME LINE

1848	First women's rights convention takes place in Seneca Falls, New York
1862	As male clerks serve in the Civil War, women workers enter the office
1870	Office workers are male and earn twice the wages of blue-collar workers
1880s	Typewriters become common in offices
	Massive wave of immigration swells US workforce
1896	American Federation of Labor (AFL) founded
1900	US economy and finance industry grow exponentially
	Most office workers are men, but 77 percent of stenographers and typists are women
	Office workers are 3 percent of the workforce
1903	Women's Trade Union League (WTUL) founded
1909	Uprising of the 20,000 garment workers' strike in New York City
1912	Bread and Roses strike of twelve thousand women mill workers in Lawrence, Massachusetts
1920	Nineteenth Amendment to the US Constitution: women win the right to vote
1929	Stock market crashes. Great Depression begins

1930s	From 1900s to 1930s, clerical work grows by more than 450 percent. By 1930, 9 percent of workers are in clerical jobs
1935	National Labor Relations Act is passed, guaranteeing the right of private-sector workers to organize unions, bargain collectively, and strike
	Congress of Industrial Organizations (CIO) founded
1936–1937	Strikes by autoworkers and steelworkers usher in new era of worker power
1939–1945	World War II. Millions of women recruited to factory jobs
1950s	Service economy expands. Clerical jobs grow by 58 percent
1952	US Department of Commerce proclaims National Secretaries Day
1955	AFL-CIO is formed, merger of the American Federation of Labor and the Congress of Industrial Organizations
1960	38 percent of women are in the workforce
1961	President Kennedy authorizes unions for federal employees
1963	Equal Pay Act passed
	March on Washington for Jobs and Freedom
	Betty Friedan publishes *The Feminine Mystique*
1964	Civil Rights Act passed. Title VII addresses workplace discrimination
1965	President Johnson signs Executive Order 11246, requiring affirmative action by federal contractors
	Equal Employment Opportunities Commission (EEOC) established
1966	National Organization for Women (NOW) founded
1967	Age Discrimination in Employment Act passed to protect workers ages forty and over
1968	Miss America pageant protest in Atlantic City, New Jersey
1970s	Twelve million women enter the workforce
	Clerical workers are 17 percent of the workforce, up from 9 percent in the 1930s
	One in three working women is a clerical worker
1970	Women's Strike for Equality on the fiftieth anniversary of women's right to vote
	Robin Morgan publishes *Sisterhood Is Powerful*
	Occupational Safety and Health Act passed

1971	Computers begin to appear in offices
1972	Coalition of Black Trade Unionists (CBTU) formed
	Group of ten women begins distributing *9 to 5* newsletter in Boston
1973	Economic "tipping point"—average American family begins to fare worse than before
	Agreement between AT&T and EEOC awards $45 million in back pay and raises to women and people of color
	Midwest Academy holds first summer program for organizers
	9 to 5 holds first public meeting in Boston
1974	9 to 5 holds public hearing, unveils Bill of Rights for Women Office Workers
	9 to 5 campaigns for rights of pregnant workers
	Coalition of Labor Union Women (CLUW) formed
1975	Term *sexual harassment* coined
	9 to 5 forms Local 925, Boston-area union affiliated with the Service Employees International Union
	9 to 5's Women in Publishing releases report. Massachusetts Attorney General Bellotti files discrimination charges against three Boston-area publishers
	Massachusetts insurance commissioner issues employment regulations
1976	Five working women's groups begin working together to oppose Ford administration attempt to weaken antidiscrimination enforcement
1977	Harris Trust in Chicago found liable for $12.2 million in back pay
	Chicago secretary Iris Rivera fired for refusing to make coffee, gets job back after protest
	Boston boss orders secretary to sew up hole in his pants while he's wearing them
	In *Barnes v. Costle,* federal court upholds first sexual harassment charge
	Three Boston publishing companies agree to $1.5 million in back pay for women and people of color
1978	51 percent of women are in the workforce

Pregnancy Discrimination Act grants legal rights to pregnant workers

9 to 5 wins "snow pay" for hundreds of thousands of employees

Working Women: National Association of Office Workers formed

First working women's convention in Boston

Massachusetts banking commissioner finds widespread evidence of discrimination

Chase Manhattan Bank agrees to pay $2 million in back pay to women and people of color

1979   9 to 5's Campaign at First National Bank of Boston yields raises and other improvements

"Clean up banking" campaign yields $6 million in raises at six Baltimore banks

US Department of Labor finds National City Bank in Cleveland owes $15 million in back pay to women and people of color

Equal Rights Amendment fails

First 9 to 5 Summer School for Working Women

1980s   Office work is largest category in US economy

Black women increase their numbers in office jobs

Growth of office jobs begins to slow

1980   John J. Sweeney becomes president of SEIU

9 to 5 film premieres

9 to 5 charges Boston Survey Group with wage-fixing

1981   35 percent of working women are clerical workers

Reagan seeks to weaken affirmative action, pulls back after nationwide campaign

Launch of District 925, nationwide union affiliated with the Service Employees International Union

Reagan fires eleven thousand striking air traffic controllers

Campaign at John Hancock insurance company in Boston yields raises and other victories

AFSCME members in San Jose, California, win $1.8 million in pay equity raises

1982   *9 to 5* TV sitcom premieres
            Massachusetts Attorney General Bellotti announces agree-
            ment with Boston Survey Group
1983   Working Women, with twelve thousand members in twenty-
            two chapters, changes name to 9 to 5, National Association
            of Working Women
            Ellen Cassedy and Karen Nussbaum publish *9 to 5: The
            Working Women's Guide to Office Survival*
1986   State of Washington awards $482 million in pay equity wage
            adjustments
            In *Meritor Savings Bank v. Vinson*, Supreme Court upholds
            first sexual harassment "hostile environment" charge
1989   Harvard Union of Clerical and Technical Workers (AFSCME)
            wins first contract
1990   Americans with Disabilities Act grants protections to people
            with disabilities
            Justice for Janitors campaign begins
1991   US Senate hearings on Supreme Court nominee Clarence
            Thomas highlight sexual harassment issue.
1992   Ellen Bravo and Ellen Cassedy publish *The 9 to 5 Guide to
            Combating Sexual Harassment*
1993   Family and Medical Leave Act signed into law
            Karen Nussbaum leaves 9 to 5 and District 925 to become
            director of Women's Bureau of the Department of Labor
            Debbie Schneider becomes president of District 925
            Ellen Bravo becomes director of 9 to 5
1995   John J. Sweeney becomes president of AFL-CIO
1996   Karen Nussbaum becomes head of AFL-CIO's Working
            Women's Department
2000   Between 1960 and 2000, Black women's employment in the
            clerical sector grows by 1,193 percent, compared to 143 per-
            cent for White women
2001   District 925 is restructured; members join other SEIU locals;
            Seattle chapter keeps the name Local 925
2003   Family Values @ Work founded

2007	Great Recession begins
	National Domestic Workers Alliance founded
2009	Rich Trumka succeeds John Sweeney as president of the AFL-CIO
	9 to 5 musical opens on Broadway
2012	Fight for $15 founded
2013	Black Lives Matter founded
2017	Women's March on January 21 is among largest demonstrations in US history
	#MeToo movement against sexual harassment spreads on social media
2020	CODE-CWA founded to promote organizing in tech industry
2021	Liz Shuler elected first woman president of the AFL-CIO

RESOURCES

Visit WWW.ELLENCASSEDY.COM FOR INFORMATION ON organizing tips, organizer training, working women's organizations, unions, workers' rights, discussion questions, books, and films.

To reach the current 9 to 5 organization, visit 9to5.org.

Check out these documentary films:
> *9to5: The Story of a Movement*, by Julia Reichert and Steven Bognar (2020)
> *Still Working 9 to 5*, by Camille Hardman and Gary Lane (2022)

NOTES

All quotes are from the author's memory, notes, and 9 to 5 archives, unless otherwise noted below.

1. Every Morning

"the messages of the new feminism": Dorothy Sue Cobble, "'A Spontaneous Loss of Enthusiasm': Workplace Feminism and the Transformation of Women's Service Jobs in the 1970s," *International Labor and Working-Class History*, no. 56 (1999): 23–44, http://www.jstor.org/stable/27672594.

"Menstruation is the special burden": Mimeographed handout from a 1960s health education class, in the author's possession.

2. Vying for Power

"Women have been the backbone": Midwest Academy, *Direct Action Organizing: A Handbook for Women* (Chicago: Midwest Academy, 1974–1975.)

"Revolutions are festivals": V. I. Lenin, *Two Tactics of Social Democracy in the Democratic Revolution* (London: Lawrence and Wishart, 1969).

3. Start-Up

"*the coming together of two rivers*": *9to5: The Story of a Movement*, directed by Julia Reichert and Steven Bognar (Premiered 2020; PBS Distribution, 2021), 89 min.

4. "I'm Not a Feminist, But . . ."

"*generally begin their careers*": Michael Korda, "Male Chauvinism in the Office: An Hour-by-Hour Report on Men's Ingenious Last-Ditch Stand," *New York* magazine, January 22, 1973.

HUB WOMEN OFFICE WORKERS: *Boston Globe*, November 22, 1973.

5. A Bill of Rights for Women Office Workers

"*articulate, coolly sarcastic, determined*": Susan Trausch, "9-to-5ers Press for Office Rights," *Boston Globe*, April 9, 1974.

"HUNDREDS OF BOSTON'S SECRETARIES": Stewart Dill McBride, *Christian Science Monitor*, April 24, 1974.

6. Teetering for Our Rights

"*Few will have the greatness*": Robert F. Kennedy, "Day of Affirmation Address," University of Capetown, Capetown, South Africa, June 6, 1966, https://www.jfklibrary.org/learn/about-jfk/the-kennedy-family/robert-f-kennedy/robert-f-kennedy-speeches/day-of-affirmation-address-university-of-capetown-capetown-south-africa-june-6-1966.

"*I arise in the morning*": E. B. White, "E. B. White: Notes and Comment by Author," profile by Israel Shenker, *New York Times*, July 11, 1969.

7. While He Was Wearing Them

"*Get my coffee, dear*": Susan Trausch, "9-to-5ers Press for Office Rights," *Boston Globe*, April 5, 1974.

"*My job behind the reception desk*": Maria Karagianis, "Clerical Power," *Boston Globe Magazine*, October 19, 1980.

THE LAST WORD IN 1970 OFFICE EQUIPMENT: Manpower Inc. Temporary Help Service, "The Last Word in 1970 Office Equipment," 1970.

TRUE CONFESSIONS OF AN OLIVETTI GIRL: Olivetti, "True Confessions of an Olivetti Girl," 1972, accessed via Lyn Peril, "Sex and Secretaires: The Rise and Fall of the Office Wife," Business Insider, June 15, 2011, https://www.businessinsider.com/secretary-the-rise-and-fall-of-the-office-wife-2011-6#1972-the-olivetti-girl-12.

THANKS, BUT YOU SHOULDN'T HAVE: Tony Natale, Cleveland Press, October 17, 1979, B27.

"The image of the loyal": Susan Trausch, "Secretaries Are Waking Up," Boston Globe, December 15, 1974.

8. In Our Glory! (Part I): "We Think a Lot of Women . . ."

"If there is no struggle there is no progress": Frederick Douglass, "West India Emancipation" speech, Canandaigua, NY, August 3, 1857.

"We think a lot of women": "Bias Charge is Filed: Against 3 Publishers in the Boston Area," Wall Street Journal, December 4, 1975.

9. A Union of Women, by Women, for Women

"What the woman who labors wants": Quoted in Sarah Eisenstein, Give Us Bread but Give Us Roses: Working Women's Consciousness in the United States, 1890 to the First World War (London: Routledge & Kegan Paul, 1983).

"I don't know," he replied: Quoted in Lane Windham, Knocking on Labor's Door: Union Organizing in the 1970s and the Roots of a New Economic Divide (Chapel Hill: University of North Carolina Press, 2017), 6.

"Harvard," he said, "is like an oyster": "The Conspiracy to Fix the Wages of Boston Secretaries," Real Paper (Cambridge, MA), February 20, 1974.

10. Se-cre-ta-REES, Unite!

"nothing in our women's movement": Susan Brownmiller, In Our Time: Memoir of a Revolution (New York: Dial Press, 1999), 312.

11. In Our Glory! (Part II): The Wallpaper Comes Alive

When a Globe reporter called: Ken O. Botwright, "Women Target Job, Pay Policy at First Bank," Boston Globe, April 26, 1979, 55.

functioned to increase *pay*: Judy Foreman, "A 9 to 5 Success Story," *Boston Globe*, September 28, 1979.

"acts to raise wages": "The Conspiracy to Fix the Wages of Boston Secretaries," *Real Paper* (Cambridge, MA), February 20, 1974.

"purely for the protection": Foreman, "9 to 5 Success Story."

12. Going National

"equal opportunity for the manual workers": Hilda Worthington Smith, *Women Workers at the Bryn Mawr Summer School* (New York: Affiliated Summer Schools for Women Workers in Industry, 1929), 256–257.

13. Hollywood

"Write a screenplay": *Australian Women's Weekly*, March 25, 1981, https://trove .nla.gov.au/newspaper/article/51771755.

"The stories we heard from secretaries": Kathy Mackay, "Jane Fonda Takes a Dip in the Typing Pool," *Working Woman*, December 1980.

"I'm just super-sensitive to anything": Joan Goodman, "Fonda: Seeking Acceptance," *The Times* (London), https://trove.nla.gov.au/newspaper/article/125651063.

"You'd go a little berserk": Kathy Mackay, "The Boss," *Washington Post*, December 16, 1980, https://www.washingtonpost.com/archive/lifestyle/1980/12/16 /the-boss/3baa33fb-459a-4976-9a09-b8772c219cea/.

"It takes a lot of money": "The Proust Questionnaire: Dolly Parton," *Vanity Fair*, October 24, 2012, https://www.vanityfair.com/culture/2012/11/dolly-parton -proust-questionnaire.

"angry complaint and immense": Lynn Neary, "A Cup of Ambition and Endurance: '9 To 5' Unites Workers Across Decades," National Public Radio, *Morning Edition*, July 11, 2019, https://www.npr.org/2019/07/11/738587297/a-cup-of -ambition-and-endurance-9-to-5-unites-workers-across-decades?utm_source =facebook.com&utm_medium=social&utm_campaign=nprmusic&utm _term=music&fbclid=IwAR17iVZNywo_zQy6sbwFY9jg4vABtPOnpNwz0g 032zzcWMaKP-1bjEzZscU.

"expected some tension": John Michael Howson, "John Michael Howson's Holly-wood," *Australian Women's Weekly*, March 25, 1981, https://trove.nla.gov.au /newspaper/article/51771755.

"There's no sense of competition": David Ansen with Martin Kasindorf, "Supersecretaries," *Newsweek*, March 31, 1980.

"No business can run": Kathy Mackay, "Jane Fonda Takes a Dip in the Typing Pool," *Working Woman*, December 1980, 67.

"No, secretaries across the country": Sarah Crump, "Jane Fonda Thanks Cleveland for '9 to 5,'" *Cleveland Press*, December 19, 1980.

JANE FONDA TO OFFICE WORKERS: "ORGANIZE": Judy Klemesrud, *New York Times*, September 26, 1979.

"a fine, lunatic villain": Vincent Canby, "Screen: 'Nine to Five,' Office Comedy," *New York Times*, December 19, 1980.

"Pleasant": Roger Ebert, "Nine to Five" RogerEbert.com, December 19, 1980.

"A lot of fun": "Film Reviews: Nine to Five," *Variety*. December 17, 1980.

"A leering, doddering": Pauline Kael, *New Yorker*, March 18, 1981.

"Preposterous": Ebert, "Nine to Five."

"Borders on the inane": "Nine to Five," *Variety*.

"Overly complicated": Kevin Thomas, "Scoring Points in the '9 to 5' Game," *Los Angeles Times*, December 19, 1980.

"Coarse": Gary Arnold, "Squandered Stars in 'Nine to Five,'" *Washington Post*, December 19, 1980.

"Male pigs": Desmond Ryan, *Philadelphia Inquirer*, December 22, 1980.

"Getting coffee," he said: Kathy Mackay, "The Boss," *Washington Post*, December 16, 1980, https://www.washingtonpost.com/archive/lifestyle/1980/12/16/the-boss/3baa33fb-459a-4976-9a09-b8772c219cea/.

14. Our Union Goes National

"women powered the new wave": Lane Windham, *Knocking on Labor's Door: Union Organizing in the 1970s and the Roots of a New Economic Divide* (Chapel Hill: University of North Carolina Press, 2017), 35.

"Sometimes workers are so fed up": Vicki Saporta, telephone interview with the author, September 1, 2021.

"It is a monumental task": John J. Sweeney, interview, SEIU District 925 Legacy Project Oral Histories, Walter P. Reuther Library, Archives of Labor and Urban Affairs, Wayne State University, Detroit.

"It is inevitable that the US economy": "The Debt Economy," *BusinessWeek*, October 12, 1974.

"missed some boats they could have": "The Conspiracy to Fix the Wages of Boston Secretaries," *Real Paper* (Cambridge, MA), February 20, 1974.

"District 925 is driving companies": Carol Pucci, "His Business Is Breaking Unions and Keeping Them Out," *Seattle Times*, November 28, 1982, quoted in Windham, *Knocking on Labor's Door,* 173.

"God didn't create unions": Alfred T. DeMaria, quoted in "'Pinkertons' in Pinstripes Wage War on Women," by Anne Field, in *Working Woman* 5 (December 1980), 69.

15. Looking Back, Looking Ahead

"expanded the vocabulary of workplace rights": Dorothy Sue Cobble, "'Spontaneous Loss of Enthusiasm': Workplace Feminism and the Transformation of Women's Service Jobs in the 1970s," *International Labor and Working-Class History*, no. 56 (1999): 23–44, http://www.jstor.org/stable/27672594.

"wrought massive change": Dorothy Sue Cobble, Linda Gordon, and Astrid Henry, *Feminism Unfinished: A Short, Surprising History of American Women's Movements* (New York: Liveright, 2015), 108.

"I thought of 9 to 5 recently": "9 to 5/925 Reunion" (booklet), September 25, 2021, available at the Schlesinger Library, Harvard Radcliffe Institute, https://www.radcliffe.harvard.edu/schlesinger-library/collections/9-to-5.

"the largest working women's organization": Ian Kullgren, "AFL-CIO Gets First Female Leader as Shuler Wins Presidency," *Bloomberg Law*, August 20, 2021, https://news.bloomberglaw.com/daily-labor-report/afl-cio-gets-first-female-leader-as-shuler-picked-for-top-spot.

"come together and act": "The Fight for $15: Proud and United in Richmond," Fight for $15, https://fightfor15.org/fight-15-proud-united-richmond/.

"tiny ripple of hope": Robert F. Kennedy, "Day of Affirmation Address," University of Capetown, Capetown, South Africa, June 6, 1966, https://www.jfklibrary.org/learn/about-jfk/the-kennedy-family/robert-f-kennedy/robert-f-kennedy-speeches/day-of-affirmation-address-university-of-capetown-capetown-south-africa-june-6-1966.

INDEX

Illustrations are indicated by page numbers in italics.